IMPERIAL TRAGEDY

Nicholas II in captivity at Tsarskoe Selo, March 1917

IMPERIAL
TRAGEDY

NICHOLAS II, LAST OF THE TSARS

By NOBLE FRANKLAND

Coward-McCann, Inc.   New York

Preface

NICHOLAS II was perhaps the most tragic sovereign of modern times. As the ruler of Russia in a phase of profound social, political, and economic upheaval and at the time of the greatest war in her history, he not only failed to meet but could not even recognize the decisive challenges which confronted his order. By inheritance, he was the Tsar of all the Russias; by nature, he was the slave of characters and of circumstances stronger than his own; and by chance, he was the contemporary of Lenin. Nicholas II represented no more than a tiny pebble cast upon the huge beach of Russian history.

But the last of the Tsars had both qualities and defects and lived under circumstances which invested his downfall and murder with pathos and tragedy. Such, at any rate, has been my comprehension. It is a personal tragedy, involving himself, his wife, his children, many of his relatives, and some of his servants, which I have sought to describe in this book.

In doing so, I have necessarily had to make some reference to the stream of Russian history and to the supreme event in it —the Communist revolution. But of such great matters, which are only incidental to my theme, I have neither original knowledge nor the *expertise* to acquire it. My object in writing this book has simply been to express and to explain a sorrow akin to that which all must feel when a blind man is run over by a car.

I have been helped and encouraged by many friends both like-minded and otherwise, and especially by Mr. Ian Grimble. I am indebted to my wife and to Mrs. Jane Degras, who have helped me to trace books which sometimes seemed no longer to exist. At the end of the book I have put a note on sources which indicates the principal foundations upon which I have based my narrative. My thanks are also due to Mrs. Lydia Bott for her translations of the passages which I have reproduced from Russian.

I should, perhaps, mention that throughout this book I have used the New Style or Gregorian Calendar. In Russia until, by the New Style, February 14, 1918, the Old Style or Julian Calendar was in force. The conversion from the Old Style is obtained by adding twelve days in the nineteenth and thirteen in the twentieth century. Also, I must confess that I have no more interest in the anglicized spelling of Russian names and words than the Russians themselves have generally shown. I have simply followed what seems to be the most convenient and the most simple. I have preferred the modern "Tsar" to the old fashioned "Czar" or the French *"Empereur,"* though the latter was, of course, generally used at the French-speaking Russian Court. Where I have quoted, I have naturally followed the original.

I wish to thank Sir Harold Nicolson for permission to reproduce an excerpt from *King George the Fifth, His Life and Reign,* Beaverbrook Newspapers Limited for permission to quote from the *War Memoirs* of David Lloyd George, the owner of the copyright for permission to quote from *Field Marshal Sir Henry Wilson, His Life and Diaries,* and the publishers whose authority I have sought wherever possible for permission to reproduce the other excerpts, all of which can be identified in the footnotes.

Photographs in the book are reproduced by permission of Radio Times Picture Library.

N.F.

Thames House,
Eynsham,
Oxford.

Contents

IMPERIAL TRAGEDY

THE IMPERIAL FAMILY OF RUSSIA

NICHOLAS I
Tsar of Russia

ALEXANDER II
Tsar of Russia

CONSTANTINE

NICHOLAS

MICHAEL

CONSTANTINE

JOHN

NICHOLAS
(Commander-in-Chief
Russian Armies 1914–1915)

NICHOLAS
(Historian)

SERGE

ALEXANDER
m. XENIA
(Sister of NICHOLAS II)

OLGA=GEORGE I
King of Hellenes

ALEXANDER III
Tsar of Russia

MICHAEL

OLGA

LOUIS IV
Grand Duke of Hesse

ELISABETH=SERGE
(assassinated 1905)

NICHOLAS II=ALEXANDRA
Tsar of Russia

ERNEST (1)=VICTORIA=(2) CYRIL
Grand Duke MELITA
of Hesse

MARIE
m. Alfred D.
of Edinburgh

VLADIMIR

CYRIL BORIS

VLADIMIR

PAUL = (1) ALEXANDRA
(2) Princess PALEY

MARIE DIMITRI
(1) (1)

(2)
one S.
two D.

HELEN=NICHOLAS

MARINA
m. GEORGE
Duke of Kent

OLGA TATIANA MARIE ANASTASIA ALEXIS

XENIA
m. ALEXANDER
(Son of Grand Duke Michael)

IRENE
m. Prince Felix Yusopov

PROLOGUE

The Seeds of Tragedy

O N May 18, 1868, a Grand Duke of Russia was born. By the Russian calendar the date was May 6th, for the Russian calendar, like most things Russian, was governed by the old style. It was, as some noticed at the time and as the child was always to remember, Job's day, and in the book of Job it is written:

> After this opened Job his mouth, and cursed his day.
> And Job spake and said,
> Let the day perish wherein I was born, and the night in which it was said, There is a man child conceived. Let that day be darkness; let not God regard it from above, neither let the light shine upon it. Let darkness and the shadow of death stain it; let a cloud dwell upon it; let the blackness of the day terrify it.[1]

For the baby Grand Duke, within twenty-seven years to be Nicholas II, Tsar of all the Russias and of Poland, Grand Duke of Finland, Defender of the Orthodox Church, all these things were to come to pass.

In 1881 his grandfather, the reigning Tsar Alexander II, was horribly mutilated and mortally injured by the hand of an assassin in the streets of the imperial capital, St. Petersburg. Nicholas' father, a man of imposing stature and autocratic temperament, became Tsar Alexander III; and Nicholas himself became heir to the throne, the Tsarevitch.

His upbringing was narrow, straightforward, and simple. He was taught to be abstemious, disciplined, and spartan; to fear God and respect his father; to believe that Russia needed only her church and her Tsar; and never to show his inner feelings.

13

His character was gentle, indecisive, and fatalistic. From his earliest years he believed that all was in the hands of God, whether for better or for worse, and this he took to absolve him from the need for decisions. Only once in his life was he absolutely certain and determined and this was when he resolved to marry Princess Alix.

Princess Alix was born at Darmstadt on June 6, 1872. She was a child of Prince Louis, later to be Grand Duke Louis IV of Hesse, and his wife, the English Princess Alice, a daughter of Queen Victoria.

While Nicholas grew up in the shadow of violence and assassination, Alix passed her childhood in mourning. Before she was seven she had lost her elder brother, her younger sister, and her mother. The light went out of her life and it never quite returned. She was always in search of consolation and for an object of human adoration. Masterful and determined by nature, she quickly matured into a girl of striking beauty. She was tall and statuesque, had golden hair and lovely luminous gray eyes, but about her mouth there always seemed to be a sign of sad reflection.

When she was twelve she went to Russia with her elder sister, Princess Elisabeth, who was to marry the Grand Duke Serge, a brother of the Tsar Alexander III, and it was then that she first met the young Tsarevitch Nicholas. A bond of mutual attraction was at once forged between the two children, and, even before they had ceased to be children, it grew into a passionate love which lasted to the end of their lives.

Nicholas longed to marry Alix. For five years he prayed to God "to give her to me as my wife." [2] But that did not settle the matter, for the marriage of a future Tsar of Russia was a complicated business. His bride had to embrace the Russian Orthodox religion, and Princess Alix was a Protestant of firm conviction. The marriage had to be approved by the Tsar, and Alexander III wished his son to marry a French princess of the House of Orleans. What could the Tsarevitch do? "It is all in the hands of God," he characteristically wrote in his diary.

14

"Relying on His mercy, I look forward to the future calmly and obediently." [3]

There followed a conspiracy of events in favor of Nicholas' prayer. In March 1892 the Grand Duke of Hesse died suddenly of a heart attack at the age of fifty-four. To her lasting grief, the principal object of Princess Alix's adoration was again snatched from her. She turned toward her brother, the new Grand Duke, and devoted herself to him but, in 1894, he married and she was alone again. The wedding took place at Coburg in April and was attended by a great concourse of royalty. Queen Victoria came with her son, the Prince of Wales. Her grandson, the Kaiser Wilhelm II, came with his mother, the Empress Frederick, the eldest child of Queen Victoria, and the Tsarevitch Nicholas came too. In a well-known photograph, he can be seen standing bowler-hatted to the right of Queen Victoria, behind the military figure of the Kaiser and beside the object of his journey, the Princess Alix, beautiful beyond compare even in the frightful fashions of the time. The Tsarevitch Nicholas had at last received the permission of his imperial parents to make an official proposal of marriage but the unanswered question was whether the Princess would sacrifice the Protestant faith. "The day after I came here," Nicholas wrote to his mother, "I had a long and very difficult talk with Alix, in which I tried to explain to her that there was no other way for her than to give her consent, and that she simply could not withhold it. She cried the whole time, and only whispered now and then, 'No, I cannot!' Still I went on, repeating and insisting on what I had said before. And though this talk went on for two hours it came to nothing; because neither she nor I would give in." [4]

Half the royal families of Europe were scarcely less than looking on. Nicholas' aunt, herself formerly a German princess and now the Grand Duchess Marie Pavlovna, added her own arguments to those of her nephew. Princess Alix's brother, the Grand Duke of Hesse, joined in the effort to convert her and even the Kaiser Wilhelm had a talk with her. Within a few days, she capitulated. "We were left alone," the delighted young Tsarevitch wrote, "and with her very first words she consented! The Almighty only knows what happened to me then." [5]

The Princess's resistance had been due to religious scruple and not to lack of passion. For years she had been as much in love with Nicholas as he was with her. "You nevertheless are mine," she was to write to him nearly twenty-two years later in January 1916, "my own treasure, my Life, my Sun, my Heart! 32 years ago my childs heart already went out to you in deep love." [6]

Nicholas stayed in Coburg as long as he could. He hardly noticed the wedding which he had come to attend, but at last he had to return to Russia and the Princess went to England where she began to learn Russian, which she found amusing but difficult. They could hardly bear to be apart and soon the Tsarevitch was on his way to Walton-on-Thames for a few days with his Princess, and there, once more, he found himself "in the arms of my betrothed, who looked lovely and more beautiful than ever." [7]

The three quiet days which they spent together boating and picnicking on the Thames were possibly the happiest and certainly the most carefree of their lives, but in almost no time they had to go to Windsor Castle to pay their respects to Queen Victoria. The old Queen, however, proved to be more indulgent than Nicholas seems to have expected. She even allowed them to go for drives without a chaperon. When Princess Alix showed her grandmother some of the fabulous Russian jewels which were now hers, she was advised not to become too proud. But in that sense, the young Princess was not and never became proud. She valued jewelry but she seldom wore much of it. Already she was devoting herself seriously to the study of the Russian Orthodox doctrine in which she was being instructed by Father Yanishev, who had been sent by the Tsar from Russia.

After a month, and after visits to Sandringham, where he found the Prince of Wales's house party somewhat baffling, and to White Lodge, where he saw the newly born son of his cousins, the Duke and Duchess of York—the baby who is today the Duke of Windsor—Nicholas returned to Russia, delighted at the prospect of his wedding in the following spring. Everyone else too seemed to be delighted, and not least his mother, who may have been relieved to think that this would be the end of her son's affairs which had sometimes caused a little embarrassment. If the Princess of his choice did not yet know the ways of Russia, there seemed to be plenty of time for her to learn, for the Tsar was not yet fifty years old.

This was not to be. In October Princess Alix was abruptly summoned to Livadia in the Crimea where Alexander III had unexpectedly fallen mortally ill. When she arrived he still had enough strength to rise and greet her and there was a formal betrothal in his bedroom. But, though his life was fast running out, Alexander III still commanded and almost everyone's attention was still fixed upon him. Not so, however, that of Princess Alix, who wrote in her fiancé's diary, "Be firm and make the doctors . . . come alone to you every day and tell you how they find him and exactly what they wish him to do, so that you are the first always to know. . . . Don't let others be put first and you left out. . . . Show your own mind and don't let others forget who you are." [8] Eight days later the autocrat Alexander III was dead and Nicholas II, twenty-six years old, *Suaviter in modo, Suaviter in re,* schooled to obedience, determined to serve, but uncertain in command, stood unobtrusively in his place as Tsar of all the Russias, autocrat of a hundred and twenty-nine million subjects.

The obsequies of the dead sovereign were seemingly endless but at last, after three weeks, the funeral was over, and a week later, on November 26, 1894, mourning was cast aside for a day and in the course of a glittering ceremony, the Tsar's marriage was celebrated. Princess Alix was now the Tsaritsa Alexandra Feodorovna. The Duke of York, returning his cousin's compliment, was among those who attended the wedding and afterward he wrote to his grandmother, Queen Victoria, from St.

Petersburg: "I do think that Nicky is a very lucky man to have got such a lovely and charming wife & I must say I never saw two people more in love with each other or happier than they are." [9]

Thus, Nicholas found the answer to his prayer and Alexandra found the object of adoration for which she had always craved and which she had so often lacked. The bond between the two was passionate, absolute, and enduring. In his wife, Nicholas was eventually to find the authority, the certainty, and the ruthlessness which he himself entirely lacked but which, before 1894, he had acknowledged and revered in his father. In her husband, Alexandra was to find the human clay for which, frustrated, inhibited, and repressed, she had waited for twenty-two years. The marriage, as the product of the attraction of opposites, was perfect, but from it, from its happiness and from its love, there was to grow a tragedy so bleak and so black as to be almost incomprehensible. Indeed, it would have been well for the two young sovereigns, twenty-six and twenty-two years old, if the hand of an assassin had been laid upon them suddenly and swiftly and before their children had been born. That too would have been well for the rest of the imperial family, for its most devoted servants, and perhaps also for Russia. Yet it was only in the tragedy which awaited him that the last of the Tsars revealed, to those who have the heart to look, the saintly qualities with which he had endowed himself, and with which he had been endowed by the circumstances which crushed him. Too weak for the worldly position which he occupied, Nicholas II was to prove too strong for those who persecuted him and tried to cast his memory into falsehood or into oblivion.

Russia was a huge enigma in which everything was approximate. Ruling it was a question not of science but of confidence, and confidence was the quality in which the new Tsar was most deficient. He applied himself manfully and conscientiously, but he made no impression. Those who had hoped for a change in the direction of liberalism were disappointed and those who pinned their faith to autocracy were also disappointed.

The impression made by the Tsaritsa was more decisive. She was not liked. Her shyness, which never left her, gave her an appearance of being haughty and standoffish. Her constant minor ailments as well as her pregnancies often prevented her from appearing at functions and gave an impression of remoteness and disapproval. Her comparatively poor command of French, the official court language of Russia, made conversation difficult for her, and though she eventually spoke Russian fluently, this took time. Her views on many things coincided more closely with the outlook of a middle-class Victorian Englishwoman than with that of the fashionable elite in Russia.

Nor was her position an easy one. Her life in Russia began as the Tsaritsa. She would have been less fenced in by etiquette if she had been the wife only of the heir to the throne. As it was there were many difficulties in addition to her shyness which stood in the way of her making friends or even making contact with those who critically looked on. And though she was Tsaritsa, she was not the first lady in the land. The Dowager Tsaritsa, her mother-in-law, came before her and when she did attend a ceremony it was usually her lot to follow the Tsar, with his mother on his arm, with someone else on her own.

It was also, and inevitably, to his mother and not to his wife that the Tsar turned for the advice and the guidance of which he stood so much in need. Between the vivacious, beautiful, and gay mother-in-law and the serious, shy, and somber but also beautiful young daughter-in-law there arose a veiled hostility which perhaps was equally inevitable. During the early part of his reign, Nicholas did not discuss affairs of state with his wife and she seems at this period to have regarded them as the separate part of a husband's life. In the same way she would walk for miles with him when he was out shooting, without herself carrying a gun. There were, indeed, some who believed that this was the cause of her later heart trouble, for the Tsar was a strenuous and tremendously fast walker. It seemed that he was always anxious to escape from those who were with him.

The Tsaritsa was not gay. She seldom smiled in public and when she did, she was seldom the first to smile. This was not a superficial pose. It was a true indication of the seriousness with which she took the life into which she had been drawn. In particular, she thought deeply about the meaning of her conversion from the Lutheran to the Russian Orthodox religion and in her quest she often puzzled the divines who had come to instruct her. At the coronation in 1896, amidst all the splendor of the occasion, she regarded herself as going through a form of marriage with Russia. Ordinary ceremonies she never enjoyed, but religious ceremonies made a deeper and deeper appeal to her real nature. The Orthodox faith, which initially she had adopted as matter of necessity, became as the years progressed, something more akin to a mania.

Her view of religion was quite different from that of the Tsar. He accepted the will of God not only unquestionably but unquestioningly. Whether it was expressed in good or ill fortune, in happy or unhappy events, in success or failure, was to him almost a matter of indifference. To the depths of his soul he was a fatalist and his indeterminate character demanded that he should believe that whatever might happen in the future was as certain and unchangeable as what had already happened in the past. He prayed to God for mercy but the Tsaritsa prayed for guidance. Her firm, domineering, superstitious, and passionate character did not allow her to accept ill fortune or failure. What she could not achieve herself must be achieved for her by God. His support had to be positively invoked and His intervention demanded. To the Tsaritsa, nothing was inevitable and everything was possible.

Here were the seeds of tragedy. Nicholas, a man of gentle disposition, had inherited a throne of which the occupational hazard was a violent death. History and heredity made him the absolute ruler of a vast empire but fate had not endowed him with the power or even the will to command. History thrust upon him the greatest decisions in Russia's existence, but character and upbringing made it impossible for him to decide. He had neither the strength of an autocrat nor the optimism of a liberal. He was made, as in France Louis XVI had been made, to be the victim of a revolution and it is a curious thought that the Bourbon and Romanov dynasties which in the past had thrown up, in turn, sovereigns on the grand scale and monsters of oppression could, in their decisive hours, produce only the negative, narrow, and nebulous figures of Louis XVI and Nicholas II.

It is also a curious coincidence that both these affable and unambitious monarchs should have been completely dominated by the far stronger characters of their wives, Marie Antoinette and Alexandra Feodorovna, and that this dominance, equally welcome to both, should have been equally fatal to both. Indeed, if there was for Nicholas II a day more unfortunate than that of his birth, it was the happiest day of his life; the day on which Princess Alix consented to marry him.

I

The Barrier

THE Tsaritsa passionately desired a son, but it was not until after nearly ten years of marriage and the birth of four daughters that she had one. The Tsarevitch Alexis was born on August 12, 1904. To his mother he was the answer of God to her long and ardent prayer. His elder sisters, the Grand Duchesses Olga, born in 1895, Tatiana, born in 1897, Marie, born in 1899, and Anastasia, born in 1901, were all strong, healthy, talented, and good-looking, and at first it seemed as if the boy would be the same. He was a large child and he developed rapidly but soon there was an ominous sign. The little bruises which come the way of every baby when it begins to crawl caused unusually large swellings. This was a terrible symptom because, as she herself well knew, his mother had in her blood the frightful and hereditary disease of hemophilia.

Celebrated doctors were called in and they were able to diagnose that hemophilia, transmitted by women and revealed in men, had been transmitted by the Tsaritsa to her son, the Tsarevitch. All that they could add was that the disease was incurable and that its results could not be alleviated by anything which medical science had to offer.

The mother's overwhelming joy at the long-awaited birth of her son was turned into a lifelong agony of suspense and anxiety, but her devotion to him was redoubled. In his frailty and in his dependence upon her he was all that her masterful nature craved.

Thus the Tsarevitch Alexis, born to the purple, was also and doubly born to suffering and to tragedy. All that life had to offer him was the test of whether he should be the victim of what he received from his father—the inheritance of the Romanovs—or of what he received from his mother—the disease of hemophilia. Here was one of the most pathetic figures in all history.

1905, the year in which the hemophilia of the Tsarevitch was diagnosed, was a terrible year in the history of Imperial Russia. It witnessed the inglorious end of a disastrous war against Japan and the outbreak of a savage revolution. It was the year in which the hand of an assassin was raised against the Grand Duke Serge, uncle of the Tsar and brother-in-law of the Tsaritsa, and in which a futile constitution was halfheartedly proclaimed. It was the year in which the Tsaritsa first began to take a serious interest in politics and it was the year in which Rasputin came to court.

Japan had leapt to the strength of a great power almost over-night but the phenomenon, apparently, had not been noticed by those who controlled the destinies of Russia. In Russia it was generally assumed that the war, which began in 1904, would end gloriously after a few swift victories. Events produced a quite different result. It was not merely that the armed strength of Japan proved to be far greater than expected but the whole military and naval machine of mighty Russia turned out to be far less efficient and far less well led than had been supposed. Inefficiency and obsolescence were ruthlessly revealed in severe defeats on land and at sea. To patriots, these reverses and the peace which followed them were a shock and a humiliation. To the revolutionaries they were an opportunity.

In January 1905 a great crowd of people, uncertain of their cause but discontented with their situation, began to march on the Winter Palace at St. Petersburg. They carried church banners and as they marched they sang religious and patriotic songs. Their leader was Father Gapon, who divided his energies between working for a socialist revolution and working as an agent of the *Okhrana*, the Tsarist secret police.

The Tsar was not at the time in the Winter Palace and the demonstration was apparently peaceful in intention, but the military authorities, either through loss of nerve or the will to

24

make an example of Father Gapon's followers, ordered troops to fire upon the procession. They did so and upwards of a hundred and fifty people were killed and some two hundred more injured. The ringleaders were arrested and exiled to the more distant parts of the empire, by which means the authorities unwittingly ensured that stories of what had happened in the capital were spread throughout the length and breadth of the land. Nor did these stories lose anything in their telling and their retelling. Industrial strife and revolutionary action followed hotfoot. The causes of it lay deeply and as yet obscurely in the past, but the occasion of it was Father Gapon's ludicrous demonstration and the equally ludicrous reaction of the military authorities.

In February 1905, the Grand Duke Serge was assassinated as he drove away from the Kremlin in Moscow. Until recently he had been the governor of the city but, hearing of certain liberal measures which were contemplated and being of a wholly reactionary outlook, he had resigned and was about to retire to St. Petersburg. In Russia, however, the act of resignation was no safeguard and the bomb which was thrown at him literally blew the Grand Duke to pieces. His wife, the Tsaritsa's sister, heard the explosion and set forth through the snow in a sleigh to see what had happened. She returned with blood on her dress and with blood under her long curved fingernails. She set out again to visit the Grand Duke's coachman, also a victim of the explosion, and eased his dying moments by telling him that his master had escaped. She visited the assassin in prison and even interceded for his life—an intercession which was rejected by the prisoner and ignored by the authorities. The Grand Duchess never recovered from the shock and afterward took the veil and retired to a nunnery. But the fate which had overtaken her husband was merciful by comparison with that which was in store for her.

Meanwhile, throughout the empire order was rapidly giving way to chaos. In the towns strikes and demonstrations multiplied. In the country, the peasants laid violent hands upon the

half of the land which had been reserved to the landlords in
1861. The spirit of mutiny boiled up in the fleet and in Finland
a nationalist movement for separation gathered force. The whole
regime, eleven years after the death of Alexander III, seemed
to be on the point of collapse. The Tsar was confronted with
the apparent alternatives of proclaiming a military dictatorship
or a liberal constitution. Most of those whom the Tsar consulted
seemed to favor the latter expedient and the man he might have
appointed as military dictator, his cousin the Grand Duke
Nicholas, threatened to shoot himself if he was pressed to the
point. As the Tsar presently wrote to his mother, "There was
no other way out than to cross oneself and give what everyone
was asking for. My only consolation is that such is the will of
God, and this grave decision will lead my dear Russia out of
the intolerable chaos she has been in for nearly a year." [1]

What the Tsar gave was, at least in appearance, remarkable.
It was the proclamation of a constitution under which freedom
of speech, freedom of assembly, and the right of habeas corpus
were granted and under which a national parliament, to be
known as the Duma, was to be indirectly elected by virtually
universal suffrage. The leadership of the government was entrusted to the able and vigorous Witte who had been a brilliant
minister of finance and who had just returned from the United
States where he negotiated the peace which had ended the war
with Japan. The peasants, however, were more interested in
land than in constitutions, and order did not return.

Nicholas became irritated with Witte. He felt that he had
been cheated into granting a constitution in return for the
promise that the disturbances would subside. He felt that it
was enough for him to give the order that the disturbances
should stop. It was up to the ministers to see that it was carried
out. He did not expect them to question his order, nor did he
expect them to ask him how it could be executed. He simply
expected them to produce the result which he wished. When
he saw that they were hesitant and perplexed, he merely urged
them to greater exertion. He wrote of the ministers to his

mother: "They talk a lot but do little. Everybody is afraid of taking courageous action: I keep on trying to force them— even Witte himself—to behave more energetically. With us nobody is accustomed to shouldering responsibility: all expect to be given orders, which, however, they disobey as often as not." [2]

But as far as any real decisions were concerned, the Tsar was as perplexed as his ministers. In essence he had no orders to give. All he could do was to bow to the advice he received even if he did not always receive it from the ministers. Even so, his conscience was stricken by the dilution of the monarchy's autocracy which he had permitted, for at his coronation he had sworn to transmit that autocracy intact to his own successor. But he did not want his mother to worry. "Of course I am not going through an easy time," he wrote to her at the end of the year, "but God is my strength and gives me peace of mind, and that is the most important thing." [3]

Another anxiety which beset the Tsar at this time was the marriage of his cousin Cyril. The Grand Duke, who was a naval officer, had been injudicious enough to marry the divorced wife of the Tsaritsa's brother, the Grand Duke Ernest of Hesse, whose marriage at Coburg in 1894 had been the occasion of the Tsar and Tsaritsa's engagement. The Tsar had warned him in advance that the penalty would be fourfold. He would be dismissed from the Navy, deprived of his income, exiled from Russia, and stripped of his rank as Grand Duke. But the Grand Duke evidently thought that the imperial bark was worse than its bite. He married his princess, and having done so, he came back to Russia and even expressed his intention of calling on the Tsar.

Nicholas was furious but within a day or two he began to have second thoughts. Several members of the imperial family and especially Cyril's parents, the Grand Duke Vladimir and the Grand Duchess Marie Pavlovna, told him that he was being too severe. The outraged Tsar wrote to his mother saying that he was beginning "to doubt whether it was wise to punish a man publicly to such an extent, especially when the family was against it. After much thought," he wrote, "which in the end gave me a headache, I decided to take advantage of the name day of your grandson and I telegraphed to Uncle Vladimir that I would return to Cyril the title which he had lost." [4]

The Grand Duke Cyril had been right. The Tsar's bark had been worse than his bite. The Grand Duke recovered his title and eventually he was allowed to come back to Russia where, in March 1917, he was to be the first of the imperial family to declare for the revolution. Nor was this all. In July 1906 the Tsar told his mother that he would *"never"* consent to the marriage between his younger brother, the Grand Duke Michael, and Madame Wulfurt, who was also divorced. Eventually, however, the marriage took place, Madame Wulfurt was granted the title of Countess Brassov, the Grand Duke was restored to favor, and it was to him that the Tsar was to abdicate the crown in March 1917.

Nicholas expected his family to behave better than they did, just as he expected his government to act more successfully than it did. He resented but could not overcome their shortcomings and he resented having to intervene himself. His interventions were of the weathercock variety. They inspired neither fear nor respect, and a sovereign who is neither feared nor respected is in danger and especially so if he is the Tsar of Russia.

The Duma, having been elected and assembled, was inaugurated by a remarkable ceremony in the Tsar's Winter Palace at St. Petersburg. The new deputies were drawn up in a group in the throne room. In other groups stood the members of the upper house, the Imperial Council, the ministers of the government, and the court dignitaries. The Tsar, followed by members of the imperial family, entered in procession. The imperial insignia were displayed on either side of the throne, which itself was draped with the imperial mantle. The Tsar and his family stood in the center of the room while a *Te Deum* was sung. The Tsar then approached the throne and read a speech. The imperial procession re-formed and withdrew. The ceremony, to which the court officials had devoted weeks of preparation, was over, but it was, and perhaps it was intended to be, an expression of the utter incompatibility of liberal constitutionalism and imperial tradition. The deputies were variously attired. Some wore evening dress, others lounge suits. Some wore Caucasian national costumes, and peasant blouses were to be seen. There were, here and there, the uniforms of deputies who were officers on the retired list, but the contrast between, on the one hand, all these varieties of apparel and, on the other, the fairy-tale, gold-braided and richly decorated costumes of the dignitaries was striking. General Mossolov, who was then head of the court chancellery and who was present at the ceremony, records that the faces of the deputies "had no friendly look" and he was convinced that the occasion had filled them "with envy and hatred." [5]

By this time, the Tsar had dispensed with Witte and had replaced him with Goremykin, already too old for serious work, opposed on principle to all changes, expert in the working of bureaucracy but bankrupt in statesmanship. General Mossolov was scarcely hazarding much by supposing that Goremykin shared the view which Count Friedericksz, minister of the court, took of the Duma. "The deputies?" Count Friedericksz had said after the inaugural ceremony in the Winter Palace. "They give one the impression of a gang of criminals. . . . What wicked faces! I will never again set foot among those people." [6]

There were plenty of others in the Tsar's entourage to expiate upon the wickedness of the Duma and the folly of a representative constitution. But of all those who encouraged the Tsar in this kind of attitude, by far the most influential was now the Tsaritsa herself. Politics and the affairs of state were no longer the separate function of the husband. Upon their outcome depended the future of her son. Writing to her elder sister, Princess Louise of Battenburg, at the beginning of 1905, she had said of the Tsar: "He has had so many bitter disappointments, but through it all he remains brave and full of faith in God's mercy. He tries so hard, works with such perseverence . . . On my knees I pray to God to give me wisdom to help him in his heavy task." [7]

The Tsaritsa knew well enough that her husband was weak and undecided. She had already spent more than ten years observing the fact. She knew that he would ultimately yield to the strongest pressure that was exerted upon him and that he was without an effective will of his own. She knew that he would cross himself and "give what everyone was asking for." But she also had the utter conviction that he had not the right to do so. The Tsar must be an autocrat and if he could not be an autocrat he must abdicate. What he could not do was to dissipate the autocracy. That would be a betrayal of his coronation oath, a betrayal of his predecessors, a betrayal of his successors and, in particular, a betrayal of her son, the Tsarevitch Alexis.

The power of the crown was therefore, in the Tsaritsa's eyes, something which did not belong to the person of the Tsar, something which he could not give away, but the Tsaritsa never intended Nicholas II to abdicate. He was to be the symbol of the autocracy, and the real impetus, the decision, the certainty, the confidence, and the ruthlessness which the autocracy needed would come from the Tsaritsa herself.

The beginnings of such ideas were consciously formed in the Tsaritsa's mind by the end of 1905 but at bottom they had been there ever since her arrival in the Crimea to take part in the death scene of Alexander III. They were no more than a logical development of the advice which she had then given to her husband-to-be: "Show your own mind and don't let others forget who you are." They were a logical development in the sense that, by her definition, the Tsar had no mind of his own to show. His function, therefore, was to show her mind.

The mind of the Tsaritsa, however, did not work by the process of logical development. It was swamped by a fanatical mysticism which overflowed into hysteria, nourished by the tragic past through which she had lived and cultivated by the still more tragic future which she had to face.

The Tsar was a willing victim of her influence and it is not surprising that he should have been. His negative and inhibited character made it inevitable that he must surrender himself to something and there was nothing extraordinary in his surrendering, not to the violent forces of revolution nor to the competing and confusing pressures of his ministers, his relatives, and his advisers and still less to the pressure of the Duma, but to that of his strong and determined wife whom he loved and who loved him. Moreover, he could not bear to see his wife suffer and suffer she did whenever her will was crossed. But her will, after all, though it was less balanced and more irrational, did more or less correspond with the precepts of government which had been drummed into the Tsar while his father was still on the throne, and if affairs seemed to be coming to a dangerous pass, that was only to be expected by one who had been born on Job's day. Indeed, during this turbulent and even humiliating period, the Tsar, as in later and much worse periods to follow, never lost the complete and fatalistic composure which he so graphically explained to his foreign minister in the summer of 1906.

At that time, the revolutionary disturbances which had begun in January 1905 were still far from over. The Tsar was in residence at Peterhof not far from the anchorage of the Baltic fleet in which a mutiny was raging. The fleet, in fact, was actually bombarding Kronstadt and the roar of the heavy guns drowned the conversation of the Tsar with the foreign minister. Nicholas, all the same, appeared to be quite unconcerned and continued with the business in hand as though nothing had happened. The foreign minister could not help asking the Tsar how he could preserve such a composure at such a desperate moment. The Tsar replied, "It is because I have a firm, an absolute conviction that the fate of Russia—that my own fate and that of my family—is in the hands of God who has placed me where I am. Whatever may happen to me I shall bow to His will with the consciousness of never having had any thought other than that of serving the country which He has entrusted to me." [8]

By those lights why should not the advice of the Tsaritsa, a devout and a devoted woman of decisive views, not be better advice than that given by a swarm of others not only less devout, but often palpably corrupt and in any case contradicting one another? There was, indeed, nothing contradictory or uncertain about the views of the Tsaritsa. She lived in a world of black and white in which men and decisions were each divided into two groups—good and bad, and right and wrong. Those in the second category had little hope of ever coming into favor or of being accepted. She had a profound distrust of the elegant and the fashionable, of the expert and the clever, but she had a touching faith in the goodness of the masses—that is, of the peasants, of whom, through the pages of Tolstoi, she adopted a wholly idealized and quite unrealistic picture. In her eyes St. Petersburg, with all its fashionable elite, its malicious gossip, and its revolutionary activity, was "a rotten town, not an atom Russian." But the people, the real people, she believed were "deeply and truly devoted to their Sovereign." [9] Her view of the correct order of things was really not far removed from that of Pobedonostev, who had taught Nicholas that all Russia needed was the Tsar, the Church, and the people.

After 1905, the Tsar and Tsaritsa came to the "rotten town" of St. Petersburg as seldom as possible. The court virtually withdrew to the Alexander Palace, the lesser of the two palaces at Tsarskoe Selo. Court balls became few and far between, ceremonies were curtailed and those which the Tsar did attend were seldom attended by the Tsaritsa. Entertaining was reduced and visitors were seldom encouraged to stay. Beyond his own family and the immediate entourage, the Tsar saw fewer and fewer people. To society and to the country at large he became a still more remote figure. Less and less he had the means of gauging for himself the truth or otherwise of what was said to be happening, and less and less the people beyond the court had the means of judging what rumor told them of the Tsar and Tsaritsa.

St. Petersburg, of course, was a "rotten town" in the sense that it was the principal focus and scene of revolutionary activities which occasionally burst into the open and constantly simmered beneath the surface. But when the Tsaritsa condemned it as "not an atom Russian" she had perhaps forgotten that less than a hundred years before her first visit to Russia, a revolution had been made in Paris; a revolution which was undoubtedly French though Paris itself may not have been much more French than St. Petersburg was Russian. The imperial retreat to Tsarskoe Selo substantially cut off the Tsar from the hub of his empire and placed him on the other side of a barrier where his connections progressively contracted. But while in 1905 there were many who came to court for the last time, there was one who was introduced there for the first time. He was Gregory Effimovitch, already better known by his nickname of Rasputin.

The appearance of this "man of God," as the Tsar described him in his diary after the first meeting,[10] was of no immediate importance and in ordinary circumstances it would never have been of any significance. But the circumstances were not ordinary and this was the beginning, not only of a psychological mystery which has puzzled every succeeding generation, but also of the completion of the barrier between the Tsar and the Tsaritsa on one side and Russia on the other, which within twelve years was to leave the sovereigns with scarcely a friend and hardly a supporter among the hundred and fifty million or so of their subjects.

The Tsaritsa had, within a year of his birth, been confronted with the fearful medical diagnosis of hemophilia in her son. But the Tsaritsa had no great faith in doctors—a fact which may have had some connection with the very early death of her younger sister, the premature death of her mother and the somewhat unexpected death of her father—and a fact which certainly had a connection with the overdeveloped mystical element in her nature. To believe in doctors now seemed equivalent to believing in the early death of her only son, and in that she simply did not believe.

She had always displayed an interest in faith healing and clairvoyant diagnosis. In 1900, while she and the Tsar were on a visit to Paris, she had been introduced to Philippe Vachot. This quiet little man with penetrating eyes was regarded by the French authorities as a dangerous impostor and he had been prosecuted for the unlicensed practice of medicine. There were, nevertheless, those who believed that he had supernatural powers both as a healer and as a clairvoyant and he himself claimed that he could determine the sex of an unborn child. Upon the Tsaritsa, who was then desperately hoping for a son, he made a powerful impression and when the Tsar and Tsaritsa returned to Russia, Philippe went with them. His prestige even survived the expressed diagnosis that the Tsaritsa's baby to be born in 1902 would be a boy, though, as presently transpired, she was not pregnant in that year. Eventually, after various rumors had spread about his political and even military interventions, Philippe Vachot was returned to France where he died in obscurity. But before he went, he played the role of John the Baptist. He promised the Tsaritsa that one day she would encounter a man of God greater and better than himself. The Tsaritsa never believed that Philippe Vachot was a charlatan and she never forgot his promise. She believed that when the need arose, the man of God would appear.

In Protestant countries, with their hygienic view of religion, Rasputin would hardly have been regarded as a man of God. The name Rasputin means literally "the debauched one," and it had been amply earned. His origin was not merely humble; it was also criminal. He was the son of a Siberian peasant. His principal occupation appears to have been that of horse thief, and his principal interest was in women and drink. But in Russia there was nothing inherently bad in the supposition that this man was nevertheless a man of God, for in Russia there was a long and powerful tradition of wandering holy men,

34

Top: The Tsaritsa Alexandra Feodrova
Bottom: The four grand duchesses—
Marie, Tatiana, Anastasia, and Olga

Nicholas II, the Tsarevitch, and the Grand Duchess Tatiana

usually of peasant stock, often of sinful past, and sometimes of great age. They were not priests but by church and people alike, they were regarded as intermediaries with God. These *Starzi,* as they were called, were often believed to have the power of prophecy and sometimes of miraculous healing, and in hours of need or of contrition they were consulted by rich and poor, aristocratic and humble, intelligent and stupid. To a *Staretz* a debauched and criminal background was the reverse of a disqualification. Nor was it only Dostoevski who supposed that a sinner in prison might be nearer to God than a mayor in his parlor. Had not Christ Himself preferred the milieu of publicans and sinners to that of the Pharisees? Were not many of His disciples men whom "Society" would have cast out? Indeed, in the Christian epoch the theme of a new leaf turned over had been ennobled and sanctified by the conversion of St. Paul.

Not all the *Starzi,* of course, were approved by the hierarchy of the orthodox church but Rasputin came to St. Petersburg with the best of credentials. Archbishop Theophane, the confessor of the Tsar, was his patron, and another imperial confessor, Father Vassilieff, looked upon him with favor and approval. He was introduced at court by two grand duchesses. Already he had the reputation, though not the years, of a *Staretz.* He was believed to have a great strength of religious vision and prophecy and, which was the most important point, the power of miraculous healing. To the Tsaritsa, shocked by the revolutionary disturbances of 1905 and agonized by the precarious health of her son, he was certain to be of interest. And Rasputin never met anyone without creating, whether favorably or otherwise, an electric effect. He had an extraordinary and penetrating stare. Those who met him never forgot his eyes.

It may be doubted whether the Tsaritsa immediately recognized in Rasputin the man of God of whom Philippe Vachot had spoken and for whom she was waiting. The Tsarevitch at the time was in relatively good health. Nor did Rasputin's introduction at court cause any particular public attention. Indeed, the British ambassador, Sir George Buchanan, did not know that he had been presented before 1907; the Baroness Buxhoeveden, who was later to be a lady in waiting, thought that the introduction was made in July 1906; and even the Grand Duchess Marie, a cousin of the Tsar and throughout her childhood a frequent visitor to the Alexander Palace, did not know that Rasputin had been there in 1905. Rasputin's name, nevertheless, was not likely to be forgotten by the Tsaritsa because among the most passionate of his many and varied devotees was Madame Vyrubova, the Tsaritsa's constant companion and most intimate friend.

Madame Vyrubova's career at court had begun two years earlier. It was scarcely less remarkable than that of Rasputin himself and to a considerable extent was responsible for it. Anna Taneyeva, as she was before her marriage in 1907, was a daughter of the head of the Tsar's personal chancery, but what initially recommended her to the Tsaritsa was the report of a vision which she claimed to have had in 1901 when she was seventeen and thought to be dying of typhus. She claimed to have seen John of Kronstadt, the priest who had knelt at the deathbed of Alexander III. The vision produced results; shortly afterward she was visited by John of Kronstadt, this time in the flesh, and soon after that by the Tsaritsa herself. Any apparent contact with or manifestation of divine intervention always excited the immediate interest of the Tsaritsa and in 1903 Anna Taneyeva was appointed to her personal suite.

Anna Taneyeva had all, and possibly more, of the hysterical mysticism which was embedded in the character of her mistress. There was nothing fashionable or clever about her. On the contrary, she was pathologically stupid, a natural underdog, without a mind of her own but with a longing to be dominated by someone else's. Soon she was singing duets with the Tsaritsa and helping her to divide the world into good and bad, friends and enemies, and eventually "us" and "them." The relationship which she achieved with the Tsaritsa was much closer and more

influential than that of any other lady at court and gradually
she came to be regarded both by the Tsar and the Tsaritsa
almost as one of their children. Especially was this so after
1907, the year of her marriage.

Her husband was a naval officer whose nerves had not been
strong enough to withstand the shock of disastrous battle
against the Japanese. On the eve of the wedding, Anna began
to have serious doubts about what she was doing. Whether this
was due to the unstable condition of Vyrubov or to a sudden
realization that she could not give herself to a man is hard to
say. She consulted Rasputin, who advised her to disengage herself. She consulted the Tsaritsa, who advised her to honor the
pledge she had given and go through with the marriage. It took
place but it is doubtful if it was ever consummated, and after
a year it ended with a divorce. Thereafter Madame Vyrubova
entered into her own. The pent-up passion of her frustrated but
submissive longings found a full expression in the adoration
of the Tsaritsa and the worship of Rasputin. She was the link
between the two.

But to the Tsaritsa the attraction of Rasputin was due not
only to his reputation as a *Staretz,* the recommendation of the
Church, and the constant advocacy of Madame Vyrubova. It
was due also to the origin and the manners of the man. He was
a peasant and, even at the height of his power, he always dressed
like a peasant, spoke like a peasant, and smelled like a peasant.
To the Tsaritsa he was one of the "real" people, one of the
hundred million and more peasants whom she believed to be
devoted to the Tsar and antagonistic to the intelligentsia. To
her, he was the most agreeable possible contrast to the stiff
courtiers, the polished ministers, the westernized liberals, and
the artificially fashionable society people whom she could
hardly abide. To the Tsar also he made the same kind of appeal
for the same kind of reasons. Both the sovereigns found that
Rasputin was somebody to whom they could talk and to whom
it was worth talking, and in their presence Rasputin, though

adopting his usual rough and familiar methods of address, showed the utmost deference and devotion.

What could be more natural than that the Tsar, who really tried to work for his people but in his isolation could not work with them, should wish to talk to one who could be regarded as their personification? And what could be more pleasing than to discover in a year of turbulent revolt and liberal thinking that this man of God and of the people was at the feet of the throne?

But beyond the precincts of the Alexander Palace the view of Rasputin was different and his behavior was also different. His love of wine and of women did not desert him and, so far from being repressed by his religious fervor, became, by a convenient philosophical adoption, an expression of it. Rasputin was intensely attractive to women and was constantly surrounded by them, but of the hundreds who came, many were brought by some hysterical enthusiasm or emotional frustration. They came receptively and from Rasputin, intoxicated with success, with fame, and often with alcohol as well, they received. To those who were ready for him, he preached, "Let us love one another that we may profess our faith in common." To those who resisted, he preached on the sin of vainglory and the necessity for self-humiliation, and to those who were shocked, he expatiated upon the saintliness of turning to filth in order to expose the halo of Godliness.

Thus Rasputin's intense religious fervor found an equally intense sexual expression and his life after "conversion" was allowed to merge with that which he had led before it. Nor was there anything secretive about his performance. Indeed, as he grasped one woman he scarcely allowed time for the others to withdraw. The technique of his conquest was that of assault rather than of approach. Outraged mothers, violated virgins, and compromised wives proliferated and did not hold their tongues. But this was not all. Rasputin openly boasted of his connection at court and especially of his influence over the Tsaritsa. A moral scandal became a political scandal and not everyone believed that Rasputin's conduct in the presence of the Tsaritsa and the Grand Duchesses was more circumspect than in that of other and not always much more lowly ladies.

Within the palace, Rasputin was to the Tsaritsa and also, though to a lesser extent, to the Tsar a source of encouragement, of inspiration, and of hope. To most outside it, and even to some within, he appeared to be a fraudulent, lecherous, and ambitious charlatan; an evil and a powerful influence. Here were the makings of a barrier between sovereign and people far more absolute and impenetrable than that caused by the retirement of the court to Tsarskoe Selo—the Tsar's village.

II

Miracle at Spala

NICHOLAS II had an extraordinary charm of manner and dignity of bearing. His eyes were gray and luminous and seemed to exude sympathy and understanding. He knew how to relax the tension which is the enemy of contact between sovereign and people. He spoke easily to simple people and they usually responded in the same way but he was also a polished and impressive public speaker, an entertaining conversationalist, and a good listener. He was fluent in several languages and could quickly and easily grasp the essentials of an argument or a report. He was neat and orderly and, though he did not employ a private secretary, his papers were always in perfect arrangement. He was an accomplished horseman, apt both in cross-country riding and for ceremonial occasions, and he was a brave man who feared neither accident nor assassination, though both were common features of public life in Russia. He was devoted to his wife and to his children. He was industrious and conscientious, generous and even-tempered. Such were the qualities of the sovereign who, through his own resignation and fatalism, allowed himself to be separated from his people and labeled by them as a monster of bloody indifference. "Between his consciousness and his epoch," wrote Trotsky, "there stood some transparent but absolutely impenetrable medium." [1] The barrier between crown and country, erected and solidified by the Tsaritsa and Rasputin, was psychologically acceptable to the Tsar.

After 1905 things improved only slowly and they did not improve much. The protagonists—on one side, the monarchy, and on the other, the social revolutionaries—glowered at each other across a kind of political no man's land peopled by liberal reformers and speculative progressivists of every shade. Rasputin's advice was vague but it encouraged the Tsaritsa in her determination to restore and uphold the autocracy of the Tsar, to disregard the promptings of constitutional reform, and to discount the symptoms of revolution. Rasputin, in fact, gave the Tsaritsa no more than the confidence to attempt what she already wished to achieve. He was the keeper of her conscience and not the maker of her policy.

Meanwhile, the chaos and violence which had come to the surface in 1905 continued to paralyze the government of Russia. Goremykin, who had succeeded Witte as first minister just before the meeting of the first Duma, was scarcely able to make himself heard in that irate assembly and quite incapable of proposing any effective measures for the restoration of order in the country at large. Either Goremykin or the Duma, it seemed, must go, for between the two there would never be any trust or understanding. This at length was appreciated by the Tsar and in the summer of 1906 he dissolved the Duma and dismissed Goremykin. In his place he appointed a man of far greater vigor and determination and of much more realistic outlook. His name was Stolypin. But while the reactionaries were enraged by the dismissal of Goremykin, the liberals were equally enraged by the dissolution of the Duma, and the second assembly, which met in the spring of 1907, was not much more co-operative than the first had been. Moreover, it contained fifty-five members of the Social Revolutionary Party.

Stolypin, however, was neither a liberal nor a reactionary. He was a great administrator with the courage to apply drastic remedies, without always relating them to doctrinaire precepts or traditions. He demanded from the Duma an endorsement of the legal proceedings which had been initiated against the social revolutionaries, and when the demand was evaded he had the assembly dissolved by imperial ukase. He then tampered with the franchise to weight the vote in favor of the property-owning class and, more significantly, with the system of land tenure so that the property-owning class might be enormously enlarged. Within four years he succeeded in getting all but twenty million acres of land transferred to the ownership of the peasants. This was done by splitting the communes, established in 1861, into individual freeholdings and by making financial grants to facilitate the purchase by peasants of crown lands. Something like order was restored and the momentum of industrial and agricultural prosperity was increased.

The effects of these great changes might eventually have established themselves as of lasting significance. For that very reason, no doubt, Stolypin became one of the prime targets of the assassins. Nor had Stolypin enlisted the support of the liberals and the intelligentsia. His methods of handling the Duma offended their principles. But university professors who used their lectures for the purpose of instructing their students in the manufacture of homemade bombs had to be restrained even if it did mean that protests were raised against the infringement of the newly won freedom of the universities.

But there was another danger which was also clearly recognized by Stolypin. It was Rasputin. Rumors of his behavior and of his influence at court spread through Russia like a heath fire. Comments found their way into the press and angry words were spoken about the impostor in the Duma. The moral reputation of the imperial family was in grave danger. It was said that the Grand Duchesses' governess had resigned because she objected to Rasputin's habit of blessing the Tsar's daughters in their bedroom, and the belief that he had seduced the Tsarevitch's nurse was not only widespread but, in view of her later confession, may even have been true.

In this situation, as in others, Stolypin acted with the courage and the decisiveness which distinguished him from all of the Tsar's succeeding prime ministers. He went to the Tsar, made a full and frank report, and then, on his own initiative, at the beginning of 1911, exiled Rasputin to Siberia and saw to it that the order was carried out. But the Tsaritsa was furious. She did not believe the reports and rumors which circulated about Rasputin. She believed that they were the deliberate invention of unscrupulous opponents not only of Rasputin, but of the monarchy. They were, after all, the talk of society which she distrusted and disliked. They were the subject of discussion in the press and the Duma, which she regarded as disloyal, fraudulent, and revolutionary. A man of God and a man of the people could not be abandoned on account of lies and distortions put about by jealous and disaffected people. Popularity and reputation did not matter. Devotion and religious fervor did. The Tsaritsa sent Anna Vyrubova to bring back Rasputin—who by then, though not to the Tsaritsa, had confessed many of his sins.

In the middle of September 1911, on his way back from Siberia, Rasputin arrived in Kiev. There he stood in a crowd of people who watched the Tsar driving through the streets. He had come to unveil a statue of his father, Alexander III, and behind him came his first minister. As he passed, Rasputin is said to have shouted at Stolypin, "Death is after him! Death is driving behind him!"[2] But this fact was also known to the chief of the secret police in Kiev, for on that same day a young man named Bogrov had come to tell him so.

Bogrov had some years earlier been a member of the underground revolutionary committee of student delegates. In connection with these activities he had undergone a number of terms in prison and he was thoroughly well known to the police. Subsequently, by revealing the names and addresses of a number of his associates, he had obtained the confidence of the police, who were now employing him as an agent. In other words, he continued as a member of the underground committee but kept the *Okhrana* informed of its plans and intentions. He now came to the chief of police in Kiev and told him that the committee had resolved to kill Stolypin and also, incidentally, the minister of education. He said that if he was allowed freedom of action he could bring about the arrest of the intending assassins. The chief of police passed this information on to

Stolypin's secretary and assured him that all precautions had been taken.

On the next evening the Tsar, accompanied by some of his daughters and also by Stolypin, attended a gala performance at the opera house. The imperial family occupied the imperial box and Stolypin sat in the front of the stalls. During the second interval Stolypin was standing in conversation with his back to the orchestra. At this moment a young man in evening dress came toward the President of the Council. He was Bogrov. Instead of speaking to Stolypin, he drew a revolver and shot him. The chaos which followed was extraordinary and in it Bogrov almost escaped. Eventually the Tsar, who had stepped to the front of his box, received an ovation from the audience, but Stolypin died a few days later. The immediate threat to Rasputin's career at court and what was, perhaps, the last opportunity of putting Tsarist Russia on a businesslike and workable basis had been removed.

Even so, the position of Rasputin was not yet quite secure. The new prime minister, Kokovstev, repeated the warnings which Stolypin had given to the Tsar. The President of the Duma, Rodzianko, came to the Tsar with the same message. But the Tsar would not act. He may have believed some of what he was told, though not all of it was true, for about Rasputin invention and exaggeration was always mingled with objective reporting. But whatever he believed, he was not prepared to separate his wife from someone in whom she believed. Rasputin's position therefore depended upon the Tsaritsa's continued support, and that support would not at this time have survived her realization that even a fraction of what was said of him was true. But after the end of 1912 that was changed and the position of Rasputin became impregnable.

1912 marked the centenary of one of the greatest and most glorious events in Russian history—the retreat of Napoleon from Moscow—and in the once heroic city the Tsar and his family joined in the celebrations of the occasion. Afterward they went to Poland for a holiday. But neither their rejoicing nor their enjoyment was long-lived. At Spala, about sixty miles to the south-southwest of Warsaw, the Tsarevitch slipped in a rowing boat and fell against the gunwale. He bruised his stomach and within a short time had developed the most severe attack of hemophilia which he had yet had. His legs were paralyzed, his temperature rose alarmingly and his suffering was appalling. His strength began to ebb away and his eyes stood out from his ashen and sunken face. He cried, then he moaned, and at last he begged for death. His mother held him for hours in her arms, trying vainly to ease his pain by constantly changing his position. The Tsar, harassed and helpless, was warned by the doctors that his son's case was desperate.

Princess Henry of Prussia came to comfort her sister but what comfort could she, who had already lost a son from the same disease, bring? Everyone believed that the heir to the Russian throne was about to die. He himself hoped so. First drafts of the announcement of his death were even drawn up. One of the doctors, Feodorov, was thinking of a drastic and dangerous remedy but he dare not speak of it to the Tsaritsa and it will never be known whether or not he applied it. Probably he did not, because his colleagues did not agree with his diagnosis. But while the Tsar and Tsaritsa devoted themselves to prayer, Madame Vyrubova was in telegraphic communication with Rasputin, half in disgrace and hundreds of miles away. Suddenly and at the height of the crisis, Rasputin sent a message. "The illness is not as dangerous as it seems. Don't let the doctors worry him." [3] Next morning the hemorrhage stopped, the pain diminished and then disappeared. Strength and good spirits returned to the child and presently the doctors pronounced him to be out of danger. In November, he returned with his family to the Alexander Palace at Tsarskoe Selo.

These are all established facts. Rasputin's message had arrived at the height of the crisis and not, as some have implied, after an improvement had begun. Madame Vyrubova was not a diagnostician and she could not have anticipated developments from previous experience, for the Tsarevitch had never previously had a comparable attack. Even those who were wholly skeptical of the supposition that Rasputin had any power of hypnotic suggestion have hardly been able to deny that there was, in this case, a quite remarkable coincidence of events. But to the Tsaritsa there appeared to be much more than that. She believed that a miracle had been performed. Nor is it surprising that she did. She was in a virtually hysterical condition and in the past, under less strain, she had believed in more improbable things on less evidence. She had tried to comfort her son and had failed. The doctors had given up hope. She had prayed for him and nothing had happened. Rasputin had spoken and his recovery had been immediate. She neither could nor wished to resist the belief that Rasputin had been the instrument of a divine intervention, an intervention which her own efforts had not availed to achieve.

Rasputin's task in persuading the Tsaritsa that the life of her son depended upon his own became an easy one, and from that, it was only a short step to convince her that the welfare of Russia and the existence of the monarchy depended equally upon the acceptance of his advice. And Rasputin did not like the Duma, which had debated his vices. He did not like its president, the liberal Rodzianko, who had spoken against him to the Tsar. He did not like the prime minister, Kokovstev, who had done the same. He did not like the newspapers, which spread scandal about him. He did not like the hierarchy of the Orthodox Church, which had disowned and condemned him, nor the secret police, who had built up files of information about his leisure hours. Grand dukes and peasants, liberals and reactionaries, archbishops and monks, courtiers and intelligentsia held Rasputin in a common hatred inspired and nourished by jealousy, scientific skepticism, frustrated ambition or moral indignation. But after the "miracle" of Spala all Rasputin's enemies were irrevocably and inevitably the Tsaritsa's enemies.

Where did the Tsar stand? He was uncertain. What he had

heard about Rasputin had undoubtedly shaken his confidence and in his phlegmatic nature there was none of the hysteria which dominated the Tsaritsa. But whatever he may have thought, he did not do anything. Characteristically he let events take their course and he, who could not bring himself to say unpleasant things to his ministers, certainly could not say them to his wife. Nor could he accept any unpleasant things which might be said or written about her. Rasputin, after all, brought her some peace of mind and perhaps he really had in some way saved the life of his son. Things had better be left alone in the hands of God. Whatever was between Russia and the Tsaritsa was therefore also between Russia and the Tsar. The "miracle" of Spala made the barrier between the sovereign and country impenetrable.

The prime minister, Kokovstev, was, at least in theory, a good Duma man and in other ways too his administration seemed to offer the basis of some hope to those who believed in the evolution of Russia and her political and social system. Impressive progress was being made with the execution of Stolypin's agrarian reforms and a broadly based landowning class was springing into existence. But Kokovstev had not the strength of Witte or Stolypin. He did not control the appointments to his own cabinet, and those whom the Tsar appointed were often not much less opposed to Kokovstev than were Rasputin and the Tsaritsa. There were also other and even greater difficulties.

The assassination of Stolypin had brought the curious methods of the *Okhrana* into the limelight and there was in the Duma a powerful body of opinion which demanded a thoroughgoing reform of the police. The atmosphere was not improved by an incident in the gold-mining district of Lena. Here, as was brought to light by an inquiry, strikers had been shot down on the orders of a police officer who at the time was incapably drunk. The name of the man to whom the Duma entrusted the conduct of the inquiry was Alexander Kerensky.

Nor was this by any means the only symptom of continuing unrest in the industrial and political life of Russia. In 1912 there were many other strikes and disturbances. Mutinies broke out in the Baltic and Black Sea fleets and also among some troops in the Tashkent area. Amid all this turmoil, there was an event which few noticed at the time. It concerned the revolutionary belief of a certain watchmaker who in 1912 was examined by the police at Tomsk. As a result of their inquiries, he was exiled to Siberia where he set up a photographer's business. His name, like that of Alexander Kerensky, would be heard again. It was Jacob Yurovsky.

Under these conditions, the third Duma pressed more and more insistently for measures of reform but the divided government was unable or unwilling to respond. In September 1912 after five years of life the Duma was dissolved and new elections were held. The result was the fourth and last Duma of Imperial Russia; the instrument, as it turned out, of the Tsar's overthrow. Its composition and attitude were much the same as those of its predecessor and in June 1913 it passed by a large majority a vote of censure on the government for delaying the introduction of reforms and prolonging the application of emergency measures and administrative law. Thus it was clear that Kokovstev, who had earned the hatred of the Tsaritsa and lost the confidence of the Tsar, had also failed to win the confidence of the Duma. He was dismissed and replaced by Goremykin, long since discredited but now more indolent and reactionary than ever. Strikes and other manifestations of discontent increased still further and the German ambassador in St. Petersburg predicted that it would only require a declaration of war to set in motion the Russian revolution.

1914 was the twentieth year of the reign of Nicholas II. Whatever the faults of his character, he was surely entitled to the claim that fate had held out an unkind hand to him. Here he was, married to, in love with, and dominated by a woman mentally deranged, almost an invalid and under the spell of the most hated man in Russia. His son, to whom he was completely devoted, was a tragic being whose life had to be measured, not by the normal span, but from day to day—a son who was lucky to have reached the age of ten. The Tsar, whose greatest pleasure was in the open air and in physical exercise, could never watch the eager activity of his son with anything but a feeling of sickening apprehension. Because he did not complain of his son's lot even in his private diary, some concluded that he did not care about it. But not so the stricken child himself. The Tsarevitch adored his father and it was only to his father's gentle word of command that the independent and often recalcitrant spirit of the boy always responded.

To Nicholas II, hardship, reverses in fortune, and suffering were expressions of the will of God. They were not subjects for discussion and still less for complaint. Any spirit of protest or revolt which may have been in his nature had been suppressed and sublimated by his harsh upbringing. Nicholas II, even when he assumed the supreme command of all his armies, never advanced his own rank beyond that of colonel, the rank which had been conferred upon him by his father.

III

War

THE Tsar hovered upon the brink of the conflagration which was imminent in the summer of 1914. He feared that it might cost several hundred thousand lives and at one moment he even canceled the order for general mobilization which he had been persuaded to give on August 29th. His cancellation, however, was ignored and within hours the Tsar was persuaded to withdraw it. His doubts and hesitations made absolutely no difference. Rasputin's advice was that war should be avoided at all costs and that war under any circumstances would mean ruin, but by the evening of August 1st Russia was at war with Germany. The event which the German ambassador had believed would release the Russian revolution had taken place, but the immediate result was entirely different.

At a service in the Winter Palace at St. Petersburg, Nicholas II, modeling himself upon the oath of Alexander I in 1812, solemnly swore never to conclude peace while a single invader remained on Russian soil. He then appeared with the Tsaritsa on the palace balcony and the huge crowd, occupying the very ground upon which Father Gapon's demonstrators had advanced nine years before, fell upon their knees and sang the national anthem with an unexampled fervor. Soon afterward the Tsar changed the name of the capital from the German Petersburg to the Russian Petrograd.

On August 6th, the Tsar appeared in Moscow. In the Great Gallery of the Kremlin he addressed a huge assembly of dignitaries, officials and municipal representatives, and also the ambassadors of France and Britain, now the fighting allies of Russia. The Tsar and Tsaritsa, followed by the Grand Duchess

Elisabeth, their four daughters and the Tsarevitch, unable to walk but borne in the arms of a huge Cossack, then advanced in procession through the great rooms and down the Red Staircase to the Ouspensky Sabor, the Cathedral of the Assumption, where Nicholas II and his predecessors had been anointed and crowned. The bells of all Moscow rang out and the densely packed crowd gave vent to storms of applause. After a *Te Deum* had been sung, the Tsar emerged again from the cathedral and was greeted once more with resounding cheers. The multitude fell upon its knees and people kissed the ground on which the Tsar had trodden. The act of going to war had brought sovereign and people into communion.

A special session of the Duma was called and the assembly, which so recently had been censuring the government, passed resolutions supporting it. Even the socialists did not oppose the voting of military credits. Strikes were called off. "In the factories in those days," Trotsky has recorded, "nobody dared to call himself 'Bolshevik' for fear not only of arrest, but of a beating from the backward workers." [1] The only symptom of the revolutionary action which had been expected by the German ambassador, Count Pourtales, was the violent sacking by an angry mob of his own embassy.

Moreover, the war started with spectacular success which filled nearly all Russia with a heady optimism. The French ambassador in Petrograd bet the British ambassador there five pounds that everything would be brought to a victorious conclusion by Christmas. After all, on the Western front, where the allied armies were going backward, the same sort of optimism prevailed, and on the Eastern front the Russian armies were going forward. As the German armies advanced westward through Belgium, into France and toward Paris, the Russian armies also advanced westward into East Prussia and toward Berlin.

The Tsar had wished at the outset to go to the front and assume the supreme command himself but he had been dissuaded by his ministers. The supreme commander was the

Tsar's cousin, the towering figure of the Grand Duke Nicholas Nicholaïevitch. Under his direction, General Rennenkampf swept forward into German territory. So quickly did the Russians come that they often found German houses deserted but fully furnished with unmade beds or half-consumed meals on the tables. For ten days the Russian advance prospered and it seemed that the whole of East Prussia would soon be conquered. To some it even seemed that the German Empire would crumble through the back door. Another Russian army, under General Samsonov, was ordered to advance in support of that led by Rennenkampf. In Berlin there was something like a panic, but Paris too was in mortal danger. In the hope that pressure would be drawn off their own front, the French pressed the Russians more and more insistently to advance farther and faster. The Russians responded and so did the Germans. While Rennenkampf and Samsonov overreached themselves, lost touch with one another, and placed themselves astride dangerous and marshy country, the Germans brought reinforcements from the Western front and placed Hindenburg in command of their armies.

Behind the German armies were highly developed, strategically planned railways and good roads. Troops could be rapidly concentrated, dispersed, and concentrated again. But behind the Russian armies and between them were marshes, forests, and lakes. Communications with the rear were poor and concentrations of troops could be achieved only slowly and, once made, they could hardly be changed. The result was the battle of Tannenberg in which the Russians suffered a staggering defeat. Almost the whole of their artillery and huge quantities of other war materials fell into German hands. Two whole corps capitulated and the Russians suffered something like a quarter of a million casualties. By October the Germans were almost at the gates of Warsaw.

On the Southern front Russian arms prospered, for here things were quite different on both sides. The Russian commander in chief, General Ivanov, was much better served than

was the Grand Duke Nicholas in the north. The army commanders, Generals Russky, Brussilov and Dimitriev, the latter
being of Bulgarian origin, were men of determination and
vigor. They were quite unlike Rennenkampf and Samsonov,
who were lethargic, irresolute and, in addition, on exceedingly
bad terms with each other. General Ivanov's chief of staff, General Alexeiev, was generally regarded as one of the foremost
tactitians in Europe, and the armies of the Hapsburg Empire
were a very different proposition to those of the Hohenzollern.
Indeed, the Slavonic subjects of the Emperor Franz Joseph
looked to Russia as the means of their liberation from the
Austrian yoke. Especially was this so in the case of the Czechoslovaks, who were generally anxious to cross the lines and fight
on the other side. They frequently did so, and in due course
we shall see the strange and unexpected effect which their
defection was to have upon the fate of the Tsar.

Many such people, among them the Czechs and the Hungarians, might now in their hearts curse the days in which they
deserted Austria for Russia, but if men could measure the consequences of their actions, they would hardly act at all. Nevertheless, and in spite of their handicaps, three Austro-Hungarian
armies of ten divisions each began the war with an advance
from northeast Galicia in the direction of the Vistula crossings.
But within a month the Russian counteroffensive rolled the
Austrians back. Lemberg was taken and the Austrians had lost
two hundred thousand prisoners and a thousand guns. Moreover, in the north, the Russian lines to the west of Warsaw were
firm against the Germans.

At Tannenberg, Hindenburg and his chief of staff, General
Ludendorff, had planned a Napoleonic blow which would
knock Russia out of the war. It had not succeeded. As from
Borodino itself, a hundred and two years earlier, the Russians
went back but they did not go out. The conduct of their troops
was glorious. They bore indescribable miseries with indescribable fortitude and they always seemed to die with a smile on
their faces. Medical supplies and services were woefully lacking

but the Russian peasant soldier seemed to be grateful for what he did get rather than critical about what he did not.

The bloodiest events in history were now occurring in France and in Poland, and all that they proved was that the power of the military defensive was stronger than that of the offensive. The war, if it was pushed to a conclusion, would be a long one, and it would inevitably grow bloodier and bloodier as each opponent tried to overwhelm the other in a terrifying struggle of attrition. The keys to victory and even to survival lay in supply—the supply of men and weapons—and the will to continue—the will of the soldiers to fight and the will of the workers to work.

Of men, Russia had virtually inexhaustible supplies. At the beginning of 1915 she had no less than six and a quarter million men with the colors. But men are no good without weapons. Something like two million of them did not even have rifles. The number of guns per battery had been drastically reduced but even so the supply of shells was "ludicrously insufficient." [2] Shooting was strictly rationed and over and over again thousands and thousands of Russian soldiers advanced under fire completely unarmed and awaiting the opportunity to grasp a rifle from the hand of a fallen comrade.

Even so, while holding in the north, the Russian armies drove forward in the south. They crossed the Carpathian Mountains and descended upon the Hungarian plain. But all the time, and more and more so, their operations were fatally handicapped by a lack of ammunition and of guns. The Germans were determined to keep their allies in the war and they came to their aid with strong reinforcements and with leadership. In May 1915 General von Mackensen took command of the Austro-German troops. The Russians, subjected to a pulverizing bombardment, began to fall back and by September their front had been driven in to a depth of two hundred miles and more. The Russians now stood on an almost straight north-south line from Riga to Czernovitch. Lemberg, Warsaw, Brest-Litovsk and Vilna had been lost. Petrograd itself was in danger. Casualties not far short of four million had been suffered. At this moment the Tsar decided personally to assume the supreme command at the front. He did so on September 5, 1915.

Bad as the situation at the front was, that behind it was worse. The enthusiasm of the first days of the war had evaporated. Petrograd was once again full of cynicism and discontent, and to that was now added defeatism and frankly pro-German sentiments. Industrial strife was increasing and though war production was growing it was really getting practically nowhere toward the object of supplying the huge needs of the armies in the field. German agents prowled the streets and frequented the salons. Count Witte, the former prime minister, openly accused the government of conducting the war on behalf of France and Britain and advocated a policy of *rapprochement* with Germany. Many believed that Rasputin, now widely recognized as the main power behind the throne, was in the pay of the Germans. Some even thought that the Tsaritsa was on the side, not of her country by adoption, but of her country by origin. The cost of living was increasing abruptly and ugly rumors began to circulate about war profiteers. Many socialists and most liberals believed that the war must be won before the radical reform of Russia could be achieved, but the majority party of the social revolutionaries—the Bolsheviks as they were already called—did not. They, on the contrary, and notably their leader Lenin, who was now abroad, believed that the absolute military defeat of Russia would offer them their golden opportunity. Nor did they simply stand by and await defeat. They actively worked in factories and in the field to promote it. Rasputin, who was not directly in the pay of the Germans, and Lenin, who presently seems to have been, were indeed powerful weapons at the disposal of the Germans. Between them, it seemed, the revolution which Count Pourtales had expected at the outbreak of war might yet be produced and, through the revolution, Germany might achieve what the frontal assault of her armies could not achieve—the dismemberment of Imperial Russia. That was the precondition of a German military victory against the French and the British on the Western front. The Russian revolution became the policy of the Imperial German Government.

So now in Russia there were three new forces, or at least forces of new design. There were, as we have already noticed, large numbers of Czechs, Hungarians and other disaffected elements of the crumbling Hapsburg Empire—men who were irreconcilably opposed to the Austro-German alliance but who at the moment, often through their own choice, were prisoners of war in Russia. Then there were the agents of the German government which was anxiously weighing and soon contributing to the prospects of a Russian revolution. Finally, there were the Bolsheviks, a small, compact, highly organized and utterly ruthless underground party which sought to control that revolution and to direct it to its own ends.

On the surface and at the time, none of these forces was of any apparent significance but it was they, in conflict and in co-operation, which were to produce the final act of the imperial tragedy.

In 1915, however, so far from being concerned with prisoners of war, German agents or with Bolsheviks, the principal issue seemed to lie, within the ranks of the Russian patriots, between those who accepted the existing order and those who demanded something far more efficient. Russia, after all, was not the only country whose system had been found wanting in the face of the German assault. The French had operated at the beginning of the war rather as the Prussians had done in 1870, and a horrible slaughter had been the result. Charging machine guns on horseback was futile gallantry. The British had appeared in the field equipped in a manner which would have enabled them to prevail more rapidly than they had done against the Boers in the South African War, but which gave them little chance against the German army. Neither the British nor the French government had remotely appreciated the industrial basis required for modern warfare; it was not only on the Russian front that a shortage of ammunition made itself felt. If some Russian generals could be criticized for their lack of resource, initiative, and imagination, so could the French General Joffre and the British commander, Sir John French. If the Russian President of the Council, the reactionary Goremykin, could be seen to be living in a different world and age to that of the trenches in the Great War, the British Prime Minister, the liberal Mr. Asquith, was perhaps not much nearer to it. And if the Tsaritsa could be thought a traitor because she was a cousin of the German Kaiser, so also could King George V of England.

But in France and in Britain the need produced the change. In Russia there were clamorous voices and considerable powers which demanded the same thing. Between the need and the change there stood, however, a more considerable power: the Tsaritsa. "The Emperor, unfortunately, is weak," she told the British ambassador, who recognized, or thought he recognized, the need, "but I am not, and I intend to be firm." [3]

The particular issue about which the Tsaritsa was being firm on this occasion was the Tsar's personal assumption of the supreme command. The decision had been deplored by several members of the government and it had caused grave concern to the allied governments. It was not merely that the Tsar, who obviously lacked the qualifications, would be unable literally to direct the armies, but his symbolic assumption of that task would mean the dismissal of the Grand Duke Nicholas in whom great confidence was reposed. Moreover, it would mean that the responsibility for military reverses, which were much more probable than victories, would fall directly, if undeservedly, upon the Tsar himself.

There was also another aspect of the Tsar's assumption of the command. Its first consequence would be the Tsar's more or less constant presence at Mohilev, the seat of the Russian head-quarters, which was situated at more than a day's railway journey from Petrograd. Thus, by going to the army, the Tsar was virtually leaving the government. His withdrawal was made far more absolute than ever before and by his decision, about which the Tsaritsa was so firm, the Tsaritsa was left alone and in control at Tsarskoe Selo. The Tsar's assumption of the supreme command amounted virtually to the abdication of Nicholas II and to the accession of Alexandra Feodorovna. This, perhaps, was the main cause of the government's concern. Two days before acting upon the decision the Tsar was presented with a letter signed by eight of his ministers begging, and indeed warning, him to reverse it. "We venture once more," the ministers wrote, "to tell you that to the best of our judgment your decision threatens with serious consequences Russia, your dynasty and your person." [4]

The demotion of the Grand Duke Nicholas, so much deplored by so many in Russia, was particularly welcome to the Tsaritsa. The Grand Duke's prestige was enormous and she feared that it might eclipse that of the Tsar. Moreover, the Grand Duke made no secret of the fact that he despised and hated Rasputin. There was a story not very vigorously denied by the Grand Duke to the effect that, on hearing that Rasputin wished to visit the front, he had replied that he looked forward to hanging him.

Ever since the beginning of the war the Tsaritsa had waged a constant campaign against the Grand Duke. "Cant you realise," she wrote to the Tsar in July 1915, "that a man who turned simple traitor to a man of Gods, cannot be blest, nor his actions be good—well, if he must remain at the head of the army there is nothing to be done, & all bad success will fall upon his head. . . ." [5] To the Tsaritsa, the Grand Duke seemed to be responsible for many of the troubles which beset the country. She blamed him for the military reverses. She blamed him for the institution of the Duma in 1905. She accused him of setting himself up as a second Tsar and there was, indeed, a story that he had allowed himself to be addressed as "Nicholas III." Above all, she vilified him for having turned against Rasputin.

When, at last, the Grand Duke was demoted and the Tsar himself assumed the supreme command, the Tsaritsa was overjoyed. "My very own beloved One," she wrote, "I cannot find words to express all I want to—my heart is far too full. . . . Never have they seen such firmness in you before & it cannot

remain without good fruit.... Being firm is the only saving—
I know what it costs you, & have & do suffer hideously for you,
forgive me, I beseech you, my Angel, for having left you no
peace & worried you so much—but I too well know yr. mar-
velously gentle character—& you had to shake it off this time,
had to win your fight alone against all. It will be a glorious page
in yr. reign & Russian history the story of these weeks & days—
& God, who is just & near you—will save your country & throne
through your firmness.... Our Friend's prayers arise night &
day for you to Heaven & God will hear them." [6]

The Tsar's assumption of the supreme command, however,
was by no means the only cause of grave concern. Nor were
members of the government the only ones who gave expression
to that concern. The Duma, now acutely aware of the breakdown in the supply of munitions to the front, had passed a
series of resolutions demanding the adoption of more vigorous
measures and the appointment of more vigorous men. Some
results had been achieved, and it was on the initiative of
Rodzianko, President of the Duma, that the Tsar had appointed
a committee of representatives of the Duma, the army and
industry to reorganize war production. Then, on the same
advice, the Tsar had brought a number of new men into the
government. Finally, and also on the advice of Rodzianko, the
Duma had been convoked on July 30, 1915.

The object of those who advocated these measures, if not of
the Tsar who accepted them, was to create what was called
a "government of confidence"; that is, a government which
possessed the confidence of the Duma and so, it might be
supposed, of the nation. But the results were not very successful. Goremykin was still the President of the Council and Rasputin still had the ear of the Tsaritsa. When the Duma met,
deputy after deputy denounced the administration and the
assembly was prorogued at the end of September. Moreover,
the new members of the government denounced Rasputin to
the Tsar, and Samarin, in particular, who was Procurator of the
Holy Synod, demanded that the *Staretz* should be separated

from the court. Goremykin declined to be associated with this advice and two days after the Duma had been prorogued, six of the more progressive and the more disquieted members of the administration addressed a collective letter to the Tsar in which they said that it was impossible to carry on the government under Goremykin. The Tsar told them that they had neither the right to resign nor the right to dictate the choice of the prime minister.

Meanwhile, the union of the *Zemstva* and of the town councils, which had been doing strenuous and by no means unsuccessful work in the organization of medical supplies to the front and of war production behind it, joined in the demand for a government of confidence. At a congress in Moscow, the councils appointed a delegation to present their demands to the Tsar, but the Tsar declined to receive the delegates. Instead, he told the Minister of the Interior, Prince Scherbatov, who was among those who had signed the collective letter to the Tsar, to summon the presidents of the two councils, Prince Lvov of the *Zemstva,* and Chelnokov, the mayor of Moscow, to Petrograd and to read to them a declaration in which, in so many words, they were told to mind their own business. When they had heard these words and realized that the Tsar would not receive them, Prince Lvov and Chelnokov declared that a break between sovereign and people had been enacted. Prince Scherbatov undertook to submit the matter again to the Tsar and to ask for a reconsideration. As a result, Prince Scherbatov was dismissed. Soon afterward Samarin was also dismissed because, as was said at the time, he had tried to bring to book the Bishop of Tobolsk, one of Rasputin's protégés.

The Tsar was now spending most of his time at the headquarters in Mohilev. There he presided at the military conferences, studied the daily reports, and spent much time inspecting the troops. Most of the great decisions were left to the chief of staff, General Alexeiev, but the Tsar kept himself carefully informed of what was being done. He established excellent and easy relations with the heads of the allied military

missions and constantly expressed his pleasure at being surrounded by soldiers. Often he brought the young Tsarevitch
to the headquarters and sometimes he was visited there by the
Tsaritsa and his daughters, but apart from the generals and
members of his family, he saw as few people as possible. Clearly,
he regretted the long periods of separation from the Tsaritsa,
but he did not regret the absence of a palace life and the court
officials and politicians that went with it. Some thought that
he was glad to be less under the eyes of Rasputin.

Occasionally in conversation with his generals he would al-
lude to the political situation of Russia but he was obviously
content, and indeed relieved, to leave the monarchy's initiative
in the hands of the Tsaritsa and not only to rely upon her advice but even simply to take note of her decisions. And the
Tsaritsa, though she now received him less openly, saw more
and more of Rasputin. Over and over again in her innumerable
letters to the Tsar, she referred to the advice of "our Friend."

With good reason, Rasputin's advice was always to resist the
demands of those who sought to establish a government of confidence. One explanation was that among these demands there
was always the one that Rasputin's influence must be elimi-
nated. His name, indeed, was now known to and hated by
nearly all Russia. There was a widespread belief among the
troops at the front that the Tsaritsa was his mistress and that
the two were in league with the Germans. Even the generals
were fearful that their military secrets would pass rapidly to
Berlin via Rasputin and though, in fact, there can be little
doubt that Rasputin did not deliberately supply information
to the Germans, there can also be little doubt that through him
a good deal leaked out to them. German agents had not failed
to insert themselves into his admiring or avaricious entourage.

Nevertheless, to suppose, as many have done, that Rasputin's
advice was motivated solely by his desire to retain his influence
over the Tsaritsa is to misunderstand both his character and
his position. Rasputin simply did not believe in the possibility
of a government of confidence. He did not believe that the so-

called representative institutions, such as the Duma or the Council of *Zemstva,* were representative at all. He could see no reflection of Russia in such men as Rodzianko, Prince Lvov, and the others. In all this he was perhaps not far wrong. Also, and with justice, he could see that, whatever they might say, such men were far too clever to be really and genuinely devoted to the monarchy. He regarded them, as they regarded him, as unscrupulous opportunists with no right to claim that they represented Russia. He may have been wrong to encourage the Tsaritsa in the belief that she must surround herself with people personally devoted to her but he was right in showing her that this could not be done by accepting the advice of the liberals. Perhaps, too, he was right in the conclusion which can be drawn from the gist of his advice. It was that Imperial Russia could not survive a further dilution of the monarchy—which, in spite of all, had its historic roots and its religious significance—and an increment of "representative" government which was not really representative and whose advocates were disunited and no more in touch with reality than the Tsar himself. The monarchy, no doubt, was to a great extent outmoded and run down, but liberalism in Russia was nothing more than an absurd irrevelance.

Nor was it necessary for Rasputin to fight for his position at the side of the Tsaritsa. It was completely secure. On December 16, 1915, the Tsar and the Tsarevitch left the headquarters at Mohilev by train to carry out a military inspection and to show themselves to the troops. For some days the Tsarevitch had been suffering from a cold and slight nose bleeding. On the journey he became worse and his nose bled intermittently throughout the day, but the imperial train rumbled on southward. The Tsar was always anxious that his son should see and be seen by the troops. During the night the bleeding became more severe and the doctor in attendance, Feodorov, became alarmed. He woke the Tsar and advised him to abandon the journey. The Tsar gave orders for the train to be reversed and they returned to Mohilev, which they reached early on December

17th. By then the Tsarevitch's condition had become critical and it was decided to take him immediately back to Tsarskoe Selo.

The long journey was a terrible one. The Tsarevitch's nose bled the whole time and every time the dressings were changed the train had to be stopped. Over and over again it stopped but nothing availed to stem the bleeding. The Tsar sent messages ahead to ensure that no one should be on the platform at Tsarskoe Selo when he arrived. The condition of the heir to the throne was always a state secret. At last the train arrived. The little boy was almost at the end of his tether and some were surprised that he was still alive. With infinite care he was taken to the Alexander Palace. Day and night he had to be kept in an upright position. The doctors seemingly could no nothing and once again he was apparently face to face with death.

Then Rasputin came. He said a prayer over the child, who could now barely speak, and touched his face. Almost immediately the hemorrhage stopped and within a few weeks the Tsarevitch was again on his feet.

Once again the skeptics had their explanations and once again the Tsaritsa had hers. Rasputin was not in danger of exile, but he was, nevertheless, and he knew it, in danger, for there were those who reflected upon more desperate ways of ending his influence.

Rasputin's presence at court and his known influence over the Tsaritsa damaged the monarchy gravely, exposing it to public ridicule and separating the Tsar not only from his friends, but even from his relations. All the same, those who believe that Rasputin's advice, which tended to keep down the Duma and to keep out the liberals, was one of the principal causes of the revolution or of the military disasters which preceded it are guilty of an almost grotesque oversimplification of history. What was leading to the disintegration of Russia was not the conduct of the war, but the war itself. What was driving the Tsar into ultimate isolation was not Rasputin's advice, but Rasputin himself.

IV

Murder

B Y the end of 1915 the Russian armies had demonstrated that their country could not be defeated by frontal assault. So far from reaching Moscow, as the French had done in 1812, it was now evident that the Germans would not be able to reach Petrograd. The breathing space which was needed by Russia for the formation and equipment of new armies had been gained—gained at an astronomical cost, but gained all the same. General Ludendorff could state with justice, "Our troops and their leaders had done their duty everywhere," but his claim that "a great step towards the final overthrow of Russia" had been achieved was a mere rhetorical flourish, the emptiness of which was demonstrated by his own account of what happened in the following year.[1]

Those who are inclined to dismiss Nicholas II's Russia as wholly corrupt and utterly rotten would do well to reflect upon the glorious deeds of Nicholas II's armies in this year and a half of most desperate and most bitter war. It is true that the faces of the Russian soldiers now wore a different expression, but so too, on the Western front, did the faces of the French and British soldiers and, on both fronts, the faces of the German soldiers. The war had proved to be more than anyone had bargained for. Moreover, it was not only the Russian soldier who began to see the frightful injustice of war which placed one man at the front to die and left another to grow rich or powerful, or at least to live, in the rear.

The Tsaritsa had thrown herself heart and soul into the war. She had always loved best those whom she could help most and

64

the pursuit of nursing had become her passion. She did not confine herself to the patronage of the nursing service, or to the organization of hospitals and hospital trains, though she did all these things. The unbending and autocratic Tsaritsa also came in person to tend the sick and the wounded. She had herself and her daughters trained in nursing, and as often as she could she came to her military hospital in Tsarskoe Selo to dress the wounds of soldiers. The worse the case the greater was her enthusiasm. In all history it would be hard to find a crowned head which devoted itself with greater humility to the often revolting task of dealing with the mess of war.

But the Tsaritsa can have learned little of what was in the minds of her patients. Her awkward and shy manner could never thaw the freeze which paralyzes the humble in the presence of the mighty, and from her attendance in her hospital and in the many other hospitals which she visited, there came no contact with the people. She must have brought comfort to some—perhaps to many—but from the upper classes at least she earned only contempt. "The Imperial prestige," Princess Radziwill has written, "suffered from Alexandra's devotion," [2] and even the Grand Duchess Marie, herself a nurse, thought that nursing was not a fit activity for the Tsaritsa.

Nor, in the view of most, was ruling the Russian Empire a fit activity for the Tsaritsa. Yet after the Tsar's departure for Mohilev in September 1915, that is virtually what she did, and a strange rule it was. The Tsaritsa did not hesitate to remind the Tsar, and to remind him constantly, of his weakness and equally constantly to urge him to be firm and autocratic. "Ah my love," she wrote in July 1915, "when at last will you thump with your hand upon the table & scream at Dzhunkovsky & others when they act wrongly—one does not fear you—& one must—they must be frightened of you . . . don't let me speak in vain." [3]

General Dzhunkovsky was the commanding officer of the Palace Guards and his crime was that he had been passing on some ugly rumors about the ill behavior of Rasputin. The

Tsaritsa knew well enough how unpopular her connection with Rasputin was making her but in his defense she was adamant and constant. "If we let our Friend be persecuted," she told the Tsar, "we & our country shall suffer for it . . ." [4] Her faith in Rasputin was remarkable and equally constant. "Our Friend wires . . . ," she told the Tsar, " *'Do not fear our present embarrassments, the protection of the Holy Mother is over you—go to the hospitals though the enemies are menacing—have faith.'* Well I have no fright, that you know." [5]

The Tsaritsa's persistent efforts to inspire the Tsar with confidence and firmness were due to her ever-present fear that while he was away from Tsarskoe Selo he would accept some advice contrary to her own wishes and adverse to Rasputin's beliefs. "God help & guide you aright, my own sweet Darling," she wrote in June, "I am much quieter when you are here— I dread their profiting of yr. kind heart & making you do things, wh., when calmly thought over here, you wld. perhaps do otherwise." [6] She utterly believed that because she had the support and the advice of Rasputin she simply could not be wrong. She strove without ceasing to make the Tsar believe the same thing. She did not claim to understand the bewildering problems which confronted Russia, but she did not think that was important. "It's not my brain wh. is clever," she wrote, "but I listen to my soul & I wish you would too my own sweetest One." [7]

The Tsaritsa's entreaties to the Tsar were full of warnings about what "they" were doing, full of arguments against "their" ideas, full of contempt and hatred for "them." "They" were the several people, in and out of the government, efficient or inefficient, civil or military, liberal or reactionary, who were contemptuous or hostile toward Rasputin. She did not want the government or the high command to be made up of men who were clever or efficient. She wished for men who were in a state of grace, men who would receive God's blessing, men, in fact, who bowed to Rasputin. For that reason, she was happy to have Goremykin as President of the Council, though he was nearly

Rasputin

Nicholas II and George V

ninety years of age and seemed incapable of saying anything
more of the war than that it was no concern of his. For the
same reason she found it impossible to tolerate men like Samarin, Scherbatov, and Sazanov in the government, in spite of
their obvious qualifications for high office, just as she had been
unable to tolerate the Grand Duke Nicholas in the supreme
command, in spite of his qualifications.

When at last, however, it became clear to Rasputin, as it had
long been clear to everyone else, that Goremykin simply could
not carry on the government, a change had to be considered.
At last, though sadly, the Tsaritsa told the Tsar, "You must
get the old man out and calmly tell him yr. decision." [8] Some
people believed that the removal of Goremykin might be the
dawn of better things to come. But the Tsaritsa's choice as
his successor was Stürmer. She reported to the Tsar that "Our
Fr. said about Stürmer not to change his name and to take him
for a time at least, as he is such a decided loyal man and will
hold others in hand—let one scream if one wishes, they always
will at any nomination." [9]

This was decisive. Goremykin went and in his place came
Stürmer. As a result many screamed. Stürmer was the grandson
of the Austrian commissary who had watched over Napoleon
in St. Helena. He had some rather grandiose ideas for presiding
over a peace conference in Russia but he had absolutely no
ideas about how Russia might be placed in a winning position.
Indeed, it was not even certain that he wished Russia to be put
into a winning position. Stürmer was widely believed to be
pro-German. However that may have been, he was certainly
and conspicuously a bad judge of men and affairs. The man
whom he appointed as his private secretary was almost immediately arrested for blackmail. The important thing about Stürmer was that he had gone through the necessary motions toward
Rasputin. To the Tsaritsa, he was one of "us" who would help
to keep "them" in order.

But even if it was not quite clear which side Stürmer was on
in the war and even if it was quite clear that he had no sub-

stantial grip upon affairs, that was not important to the Tsaritsa. She did not, in any case, expect ministers to take any initiative. She expected them to carry out instructions. She also expected that God would smile on Russia if appointments were given to men recommended by Rasputin, for now, in the advancing stage of her mystical hysteria, she was having difficulty in distinguishing between Rasputin and Christ. The Tsar, before coming to decisions, was exhorted to stroke his hair with a comb supplied by Rasputin. To the Tsaritsa, it was more important that a minister should be acceptable in the sight of God than that he should understand the railway system of Russia or the processes by which more armaments might be manufactured.

Her faith was wonderful. She was undismayed by the worst crises. She did not, as she repeatedly told the Tsar, know about things, but she had "feelings" about them and she never for a moment doubted that her feelings were right. She consulted Rasputin about everything and listened to his advice about everything, ranging from minor appointments to the major strategic conduct of the war. And always the result of her feelings was the same. Good fortune would come from taking Rasputin's advice. Disaster would come from disregarding it. No concessions must be made to pressure from the Duma or elsewhere. The Tsar must be firm. The autocracy must be preserved. If only the Tsar would do as he was told by her, she could still foresee a glorious reign ahead of him and of their son. Without concealment, she treated her husband like a mother's adorable but slightly unreliable child, and that on the whole was the manner in which he responded to her treatment. The Tsar, in fact, had virtually gone into a coma—so much so, indeed, that some believed he was being systematically drugged by Rasputin.

As the summer of 1916 drew to an end, the Tsaritsa resolved to have a new minister of the interior. The man upon whom her choice had fallen was Protopopov. The important thing about Protopopov was that he was suffering from a form of creeping paralysis and had submitted himself to the mystical treatments of Rasputin, in whom he professed to recognize the man of God so dear to the Tsaritsa. His other qualifications were less impressive and his background was a curious one for a favorite of the Tsaritsa's. He had been elected to the Duma and had achieved the position of vice-president of it in the guise of moderate liberalism. In the summer of 1916 he had led a delegation of the Duma on good-will visits to England and France but on the way back, as was soon widely known, he had a series of rather compromising discussions with a German agent in Stockholm. His life's ambition had been to become a vice-governor; now he was to do better than that. His appointment caused a storm of abuse. To most patriots he appeared to be a traitor. By the liberals he was regarded not merely as an enemy but as a turncoat. By almost everybody he was thought to be wholly incompetent. The government of Russia seemed to have come to its lowest point. With Stürmer as its prime minister and Protopopov as its minister of the interior, it was not even quite clear which side it was on in the war. And the people now more than ever had cause to give vent to their dissatisfaction.

Prices were going up. Transport was breaking down. The Tsar was told that people were beginning to starve. He decided not to consult the Tsaritsa. He decided to act. He found it strange that people had no confidence in Stürmer, but he saw that they did not have that confidence. He did not understand why the distribution of food was breaking down, but he did see that it was breaking down. He knew that the Tsaritsa was full of faith and confidence, but he was not himself full of that faith and confidence. "I am receiving St[ürmer] in an hour," he wrote to the Tsaritsa from Mohilev on November 22, 1916, "and shall insist on his taking leave." [10]

This unusually decisive and even abrupt decision of the Tsar's brought a "big lump" to the Tsaritsa's throat. She had regarded Stürmer as "such a devoted, honest, sure man." She regretted his departure "because he likes our Friend and was so right in that way." She did not like the new prime minister, Trepov, and could never have the same feeling for him as she had for "old Goremykin & Stürmer—they were of the good old sort." She doubted whether Trepov cared for her and she foresaw that "if he does not trust me or our Friend things will be difficult." At least, however, she had arranged for Stürmer to tell Trepov "how to behave about Gregory & to safeguard him always."[11]

But the new prime minister, Trepov, had already decided how to "behave" about Gregory. What he had decided was not surprising but the way in which he sought to achieve it makes, even for the closing months of the Romanov dynasty, one of the strangest stories. This was the situation: Almost the whole articulate public opinion of Russia was in a state of uproar about occult influences in high places, and there was an immediate prospect of starvation and unemployment through the rise in prices and the failure of the transport system. Public anger appeared to be focussed upon Stürmer, the outgoing prime minister, but his successor rightly diagnosed that it could not be appeased simply by a change of prime ministers. He knew that the real target of attack was Rasputin. Trepov was determined to form a government, if not of confidence, of independence; that is, independent of Rasputin. And he thought he had a chance of doing so. The Tsar was still at his headquarters in Mohilev. The Tsaritsa was in Tsarskoe Selo and the Tsar, by dismissing Stürmer, had already shown that the gravity of the situation had not escaped him.

Trepov's first task was to get rid of Protopopov, the Minister of the Interior. This, indeed, was the key to the whole business. Protopopov was an abject creature of Rasputin's—a symbol as also an agent of his political power. Trepov discussed the matter with the Tsar at Mohilev and he seemed to gain all that he could have wished. The Tsar agreed to the dismissal of Protopopov and he also agreed to a number of other important changes. Once again, he did so without consulting the Tsaritsa. Indeed, he now seemed to have emerged from his coma and to have propelled himself into the kind of action which the Tsaritsa had so often urged but perhaps not expected. "I am sorry for Prot. [opopov]," he wrote to the Tsaritsa on November 23rd, "—he is a good, honest man, but he jumps from one idea to another and cannot make up his mind on anything. I noticed that from the beginning. They say that a few years ago he was not quite normal after a certain illness. . . . It is risky to leave the Ministry of Internal Affairs in the hands of such a man in these times!" Nor was this all that the Tsar had to say to his wife. "Only, I beg you," he added, "do not drag our Friend into this. The responsibility is with me, and therefore I wish to be free in my choice." 12

For Nicholas II this was an outburst and an extraordinary outburst at that. For more than twenty years he had gladly deferred to his wife. His constant aim had been to do nothing which would cause her pain or displeasure. For her sake, he had repeatedly sacrificed his own better judgment. For her peace of mind, he had given up his own. For her love, he had abandoned his friends, many of his activities and even the greater part of his imperial function. But now, not in anger and certainly not in revenge, he struck out at the very root of her beliefs. Worn down by strain and anxiety to a parody of his former appearance, he raised himself to save Russia—to save Russia from his wife. "Only, I beg you," he had said, "do not drag our Friend into this."

But the Tsaritsa, so full of love for her husband, was without compassion for him and without any conviction that his judgment was right. Blind to political reality, blind to the crisis of Russia, and blind to the agony of the Tsar, she could submit only to the hysterical promptings of her extraordinary nature. "Forgive me, deary, believe me—I entreat you," she wrote from Tsarskoe Selo, "dont go and change Protopopov now, he will be alright, give him the chance to get the food supply matter into his hands & I assure you, all will go. . . . Oh, Lovy, you can trust me. I may not be clever enough—but I have a strong feeling & that helps more than the brain often." Nor did the

Tsaritsa miss the main point of what the Tsar was doing. "Once more, remember," she wrote, "that for your reign, Baby & us you need the strength prayers & advice of our Friend. . . . Protopopov venerates our Friend & will be blessed." [13] Nor did she even pay lip service to the Tsar's wish to be "free" in his own choice. "Darling, remember," she told him, "that it does not lie in the man Protopopov or X.Y.Z., but its the question of monarchy and yr. prestige now, which must not be shattered in the time of the Duma. Dont think they will stop at him, but they will make all others leave who are devoted to you one by one—& then ourselves." [14] Nor was the Tsaritsa content only with sending letters. She came herself to Mohilev to talk things over "quietly." Protopopov was saved, and Trepov was back at the point from which he had started. In dealing separately with the Tsar, the new prime minister had underestimated the Tsaritsa.

Trepov, all the same, still had, or thought he had, a card up his sleeve. He knew and he knew that Rasputin knew the great physical danger in which the *Staretz* now stood. The loathing of him was almost universal and there was a general feeling that anybody who killed Rasputin would be committing not murder but a public service. Perhaps, Trepov concluded, the *Staretz* might be induced to consider the advantage of a secure retirement. At any rate he determined to find out. As his emissary he chose his brother-in-law, General Mossolov, who was head of the Tsar's chancellery.

General Mossolov, as a court official, was in a delicate position. But he was also in difficulty because whenever he sought out Rasputin, he seemed to find him incapably drunk and hardly ready to discuss business. At last, however, an opportunity arose. On behalf of the prime minister, General Mossolov offered him two hundred thousand rubles in cash, a house in Petrograd, all his living expenses, and the provision of a strong bodyguard. These payments in cash, in kind, and in services were to be made on the day of Protopopov's resignation from the government and in return for a guarantee from Rasputin that he would restrict his influence over the Tsaritsa to the question of church appointments.

Here, then, was a curious position. A high court official, on behalf of the prime minister, was trying to bribe the Tsaritsa's favorite so that the Tsar's decision, which had been reversed by the Tsaritsa, could be carried out after all. Moreover, the bribe itself was absurd. Why should Rasputin have coveted two hundred thousand rubles when he could easily have made two million? Why should he want a house when, if he had wanted it, he could have had a palace? Why should he want a bodyguard when the Supreme Commander of all the Russian armies had to lean on his advice? Why should he abandon his protégé in the government when he could readily—and especially now—unseat the prime minister? It is hardly surprising that Trepov did not long survive in his high position or that the Tsar presently sent General Mossolov abroad to a diplomatic appointment. Protopopov remained as the Minister of the Interior.

The Tsar had made his last stand. Now he simply had to adjust himself to the danger of leaving Protopopov at the head of affairs in the Ministry of the Interior. The Tsaritsa and Rasputin had triumphed. It seemed that there could be no escape from their power and those, including perhaps the Tsar himself, who had hoped for changes after the dismissal of Stürmer were bitterly disappointed. And in these circumstances of utter frustration it was almost inevitable that people's minds should turn more and more to thoughts of violence. In Petrograd the talk was of a revolution from above and innumerable plots of different kinds were discussed. Some thought a complete palace revolution leading to the proclamation of a new Tsar was needed. Others thought that the removal of the Tsaritsa would be enough but, like so much else in Russia, all this was simply talk. Nothing took definite shape, nothing was done, and nothing was attempted. Three ultra-monarchists, all the same, had resolved that Rasputin must be killed.

One, named Purishkevich, was a member of the Duma who

represented the extreme right wing of that assembly, and had at least as much contempt for the liberals as the Tsaritsa herself. Another was Prince Felix Yusopov, the son of one of the greatest landowners in Russia and the husband of one of the Tsar's nieces. The third, apparently, was the Grand Duke Dimitri, son of the Tsar's uncle, the Grand Duke Paul. The aim of the plot was the same as that of the bribery attempt which had been made by Trepov; namely, to free the government from the influence of Rasputin and of the Tsaritsa. The plotters, with not much more foresight than Trepov, believed that after Rasputin's death, the Tsaritsa would soon have to retire to a mental home, and that the Tsar would recognize their good intentions because of their exalted rank. Indeed, the twenty-six-year-old Grand Duke Dimitri was permitted to address the Tsar as "Uncle" and since he had lost his mother in early childhood, he had always been regarded both by the Tsar and the Tsaritsa almost as a son of their own.

The plan was prepared with considerable skill but executed with somewhat less expedition. At midnight on December 29, 1916, Prince Felix Yusopov lured Rasputin to a cellar in the Yusopov house on the pretext of introducing him to his wife, who was actually in the Crimea. In a room above, the other conspirators sat waiting. A gramophone played loud music. In the cellar, Prince Yusopov gave Rasputin several cakes and glasses of wine which had been carefully treated with cyanide of potassium. After a hesitant start which almost caused Yusopov to abandon the plan, Rasputin ate and drank freely, but the poison seemed to have no effect and after a time Rasputin asked Yusopov to play his guitar. While the murderer played and sang, the victim enjoyed himself. At last, Yusopov found a pretext to withdraw and went up to consult with his friends. It is said that the Grand Duke Dimitri was ready to give in but that Purishkevich was determined to persevere. Yusopov returned to the cellar with the Grand Duke's revolver concealed behind his back, convinced that he had to deal with the supernatural. This he did by firing point-blank into Rasputin's back

74

near the heart. The *Staretz* fell and the other conspirators came down to survey the night's work. All were convinced that their victim was stone-dead.

The Grand Duke Dimitri now left with another man dressed like Rasputin to create a blind. Purishkevich and Yusopov stayed talking upstairs for some time and presently Yusopov returned again to the cellar. There the body still lay, but as he looked at it, Rasputin suddenly staggered to his feet, grasped his assailant by the shoulder and fell again. Yusopov fled in terror. Rasputin crawled out of the house and into the snow roaring in agony or in rage. Purishkevich went after him firing several shots. At last he kicked him on the head and with the help of two soldiers who happened to be nearby, dragged the body back into the house. It was then tied up and taken to a *drowned* bridge and dropped through a hole in the ice into the river Neva. When it was recovered on January 1, 1917, it was noticed that one arm had worked itself loose from the bindings and that the hand seemed to be making the sign of the cross. Rasputin in his death was hardly less remarkable than he had been in his life.

In effect the Russian revolution had begun. The opening moves had been made by a right-wing deputy, a prince, and a grand duke. The murder in the cellar of Yusopov's house was soon to find, as Rasputin himself had expected, a counterpart in another celler of Ipatiev's house on the other side of Russia.

V

Revolution

THE killing of Rasputin was a hopeless fiasco. Morally it was a crime. Politically it was a miscalculation. Psychologically it was a blunder. The intention of the plotters was to remove what they conceived to be the power behind the Tsaritsa and thus to eliminate the Tsaritsa herself as a force in the government of Russia. In this way, they hoped to liberate the Tsar and to leave him in a position in which he would choose, or at least could be forced to accept, new men in the government and to adopt new measures of governance. The intention also was that the Tsar should be able to stand forth again as sovereign in his own right, cleansed of what had become the smear of occult influences, and that the Russian people should gain a sense of recompense in place of the pent-up and frustrated hatred which they had apparently felt against Rasputin.

The last part of the plan, which was its most realistic and its most dangerous aspect, was to a great extent realized. When people heard that Rasputin was dead, they embraced one another in the streets. The plotters themselves became popular national heroes. But for the rest, the plan miscarried in every possible respect. The plan and all those who saluted its achievement had completely miscalculated the character of the Tsaritsa, the position of Rasputin, and the reaction of the Tsar.

Rasputin was not a policy maker. His advice was a careful and, no doubt, a studied reflection of what was already in the Tsaritsa's mind. He did not form her judgment. He gave her confidence in the judgment she had already formed. He constantly put forward and secured the appointment of his own candidates for office in state, church, and army, but his death removed nothing significant from the power or the confidence of the Tsaritsa. The faith which she had in his blessing during his lifetime she also had in what she regarded as his blessing after his death. Moreover, Rasputin's advice to the Tsaritsa had more often than not been conveyed to her, not by word of mouth, but in the form of messages sent either by telegrams or through the mediation of Madame Vyrubova. After his death these messages did not have to cease, for the spirit of Rasputin was considered to be very much alive. Moreover, what was considered to be an inspiration from a saint in heaven was liable to create an even greater effect than what had previously been a mere message or telegram from a saint on earth. The influence of Madame Vyrubova, great before the death of Rasputin, became greater still after it. Similarly the power of Protopopov was also increased, for Protopopov had little difficulty in convincing the Tsaritsa that he was as closely in touch with Rasputin in heaven as he had been with him on earth. The advice of Madame Vyrubova and Protopopov was more purblind, less imaginative, but not less influential than that of Rasputin had been.

Nor was that all. The Tsaritsa had long since drawn hard and fast lines between the good men and the bad men, between those who venerated Rasputin and those who did not, between "us" and "them." "They," she believed, could not be blessed in the sight of God, could not be crowned with success, and ought not to be appointed to office by the Tsar. "They," the Tsaritsa believed, were evil, unclean, and wicked, but her conviction had by no means been entirely shared by the Tsar. After the death of Rasputin, however, the Tsaritsa could show that they were more than wicked. She could also claim that they were criminal, for she could identify them with crime and with the crime of murder at that. The black and white into which the Tsaritsa divided men and affairs became, after Rasputin's death, blacker and whiter. Protopopov became more dear to her and the Duma became more hateful.

Then also, the Tsaritsa had long since become convinced that the life of her son and the future of the dynasty were identified with and dependent upon the life of Rasputin. This was a desperate and hysterical kind of belief possible only for a tortured woman. The death of Rasputin could only make her more desperate, more hysterical, more tortured and, as well, much more bitter and even more violent than she had been before. Those who expected that Rasputin's death would cause her collapse, and perhaps even her retirement to a mental home, were rudely shocked.

As to the reaction of the Tsar himself, there was also a complete miscalculation. The idea of liberating him from the Tsaritsa was absurd, and if the inner development of the crisis between Tsar and Tsaritsa over the proposed dismissal of Protopopov in November and December 1916 had been known, would have been obviously absurd.

No one will ever know exactly what passed between the two sovereigns at Mohilev in those crucial days. There was, it is certain, no estrangement between them. Both were still intoxicated with each other as though they were a honeymoon couple. But it is equally certain that there was a trial of strength between their characters which the Tsaritsa won easily, completely, and enduringly. When she left to return to Tsarskoe Selo, the Tsar wrote to her referring to the difficulties of the days through which they had just lived, "but only thanks to you," he said, "have I spent them more or less calmly. You were so strong and steadfast," he added, "—I admire you more than I can say." [1]

While the Tsar was writing these words to her, the Tsaritsa was writing to him. "I am fully convinced," she said, "that great & beautiful times are coming for yr. reign & Russia. Only keep up your spirits, let no talks or letters pull you down— let them pass by as something unclean & quickly to be forgotten. Show to all, that you are the master & your will shall be obeyed —the time of great indulgence & gentleness is over—now comes your reign of will & power, & they shall be made to bow down

78

before you & listen [to] your orders & to work how & with whom you wish—obedience they must be taught, they do not know the meaning of that word, you have spoilt them by yr. kindness & all forgivingness. Why," the Tsaritsa asked as she came to the real point, "do people hate me? Because they know I have a strong will & when [I] am convinced of a thing being right (when besides [I am] blessed by Gregory), do not change my mind & that they can't bear."

The Tsaritsa went on to remind the Tsar of the bell and image which she had been given by Philippe Vachot. The bell and image, she had been told by Philippe, would enable her to distinguish good men from bad. "As you were so kind, trusting & gentle, I was to be yr. bell," she told the Tsar, "those that came with wrong intentions wld. not be able to approach me & I wld. warn you." She then warned him against "the black ones," among whom the prime minister, Trepov, was listed, and she even warned him to disregard the letters which he might receive from his mother, the dowager Tsaritsa Marie Feodorovna. "Thank God, she is not here," the Tsaritsa wrote, "but kind people find means of writing & doing harm." [2]

These were not the words of a woman who would easily crumple up even when confronted with the worst of disasters. Nor was the Tsar in a frame of mind which made it likely that he would seize any opportunity to assert his authority against that of his wife. His reply to her letter came in the form of a telegram. "Have arrived safely," it said. "A lovely clear day; 2° of frost. Thank you once more for dear letter. Hope you are feeling well. Both kiss you tenderly." [3]

The Tsar, in fact, had returned to his state of political coma. His preoccupation was with the military preparation of the great offensive which was to start in the spring of 1917. The comparative inactivity of 1916 had enabled the great Russian armies to regroup and to expand. The forces were better trained and much better equipped than they had been in 1915. The German military offensive had shot its bolt and the Austrian had more than shot its bolt. In the Russian high command, there was a growing feeling that the dawn of victory was approaching. If the Tsar judged that such a victory would change everything he was quite right, but in judging, as he undoubtedly did, that the Tsaritsa could manage the rear, the political base upon which the military offensive must depend, he was quite wrong. If, in view of his character and of hers, there was any alternative to that judgment, there was certainly no alternative to it after the death of Rasputin. The murder of the *Staretz,* so far from creating an opportunity for the "restoration" of Nicholas II, removed any possibility of such a thing. It left Russia with the choice between the autocracy of Alexandra Feodrovna and the revolutionary overthrow of the monarchy. There could no longer be much doubt about what the choice would be. In prophesying that if he was struck down by aristocrats, the Romanov dynasty would in turn be struck down by the people, Rasputin was really making no more than a sound appraisal of the political certainties in Russia. The seeds of tragedy had come to maturity. Russia was on the brink of unspeakable horrors. The imperial family was at the threshold of persecution and of martyrdom. But perhaps also Russia, which was staggering from defeat to disaster, was on the eve of her greatest era and certainly the imperial family, which was now sinking with the wreck of the Tsar's reign, was yet to reveal a nobility and a Christian heroism which was still unseen and unsuspected. For the Tsar, the Tsaritsa, their four daughters, and their fragile little son, the "great and beautiful times" of which the Tsaritsa had written, though not of the kind which she had expected, were nevertheless almost at hand. But before the heights could be reached, the depths had to be plumbed.

When the Tsar heard of the murder of Rasputin he was "horrified and shaken." [4] At once he left his headquarters to return to Tsarskoe Selo. There were those who believed that he was glad and relieved to be done once and for all, as he might have expected, with Rasputin. But whether this was so or not, he certainly could not be glad to be confronted by his wife in her now more than ever desperate and hysterical condition. Nor, in spite of, and indeed because of, their popularity, could he countenance the plotters though one was his nephew by marriage and another was the son of his uncle and, in spirit, a son of his own.

There was not much doubt about who the plotters were. Even before Rasputin's body had been dredged up out of the river Neva to prove that a crime had been committed, the fact and the identity of those who had done it was a matter of common knowledge. On the first day after the event, the Tsaritsa knew that Prince Felix Yusopov had taken Rasputin to his house during the previous night. She knew that the Grand Duke Dimitri and the deputy Purishkevich had been in the house at the time. She knew that in the night Purishkevich "ran out screaming to the Police that our Friend was killed." [5]

Prince Felix Yusopov at first denied that he had anything to do with the crime but presently he dropped that rather transparent claim. The Grand Duke Dimitri merely denied that he had actually struck the death blow. He did not deny that he was one of the conspirators or that he was in the Yusopov house at the time of the execution. Within the imperial family a series of extraordinary tensions was created. In the household of the Tsar's uncle, the Grand Duke Paul, there was, for example, a curious situation. The Grand Duke, who had recently established very friendly relations with the Tsaritsa, was himself the father by his first marriage of one of those involved, but the elder sister of his second wife, Princess Paley, was one of Rasputin's most fanatical admirers. Moreover, one of Princess Paley's sons by her first marriage was the husband of Madame Vyrubova's sister. But another of Princess Paley's children by her first marriage was among the closest of the Grand Duke Dimitri's friends. Then there was the complication that the Grand Duke Dimitri had apparently consulted the Grand Duchess Elisabeth, the Tsaritsa's sister, about the conspiracy and also apparently had been encouraged by her to persist in it and even to regard the murder as part of God's work.

Most of the imperial family, nevertheless, was united in the belief that the Tsar, so to speak, should capitalize the popularity which was being enjoyed by Rasputin's assassins. On the initiative of the Grand Duchess Marie Pavlovna, the widow of Alexander II's third son and the most colorful member of the imperial family, a petition to the Tsar was drawn up in which it was urged that the Grand Duke Dimitri and Prince Felix Yusopov should both receive a free pardon. The Grand Duchess Marie Pavlovna hated the Tsaritsa, but the petition was submitted to the Tsar by the Grand Duke Paul himself. The Tsar returned it with the comment that murder could not be overlooked.

No very severe punishment, all the same, fell upon the principal conspirators. Prince Felix Yusopov was banished to one of his estates and the Grand Duke Dimitri was dispatched to one of the more obscure battle fronts. The penalty for killing Rasputin proved to be no greater than that which had previously been meted out to several exalted persons for criticizing him. Russia noted that the Tsar looked with disfavor upon the heroes who had rid him of Rasputin, but Russia also noted the feeble expression which was given to the sovereign's wrath. The cost of murdering the Tsaritsa's favorite was evidently not very high.

Meanwhile, Protopopov, now utterly secure in office, was getting the matter of the food supply into his hands. The results of his activities were not very successful. In fact, it was becoming clear to most that Petrograd was on the point of starvation. It was not that there was any shortage of food in Russia, but the means of distributing it were breaking down. As a result, the prices of what was available were soaring to impossible heights. Moreover, the breakdown of transport which was causing this shortage of food and the resulting inflation was also creating a shortage of fuel not only for domestic but also for industrial purposes. Unemployment was spreading, and in Petrograd people were not only beginning to grow hungry but they were also beginning to be confronted with an enforced idleness. In addition, there were in Petrograd at least 150,000 half-trained army recruits who, as a result of equipment shortages, had little to do and plenty to think about.

This was clearly a dangerous and even an explosive situation, but whether Protopopov's failure to deal with it was entirely due to the increasing paralysis of his brain was not quite clear. There were many who believed that he was engaged deliberately in a great inflation of the police provocation method. The theory was that his conversation with a German agent in Stockholm when on the way back from England had not been undertaken in a fit of absent-mindedness and that it was not an isolated incident. The theory was that Protopopov had genuine pro-German sympathies and that he was working for the establishment of a separate peace between Russia and Germany.

If so, Protopopov was in a difficult situation, for the Tsar was resolute in his determination to continue the war until victory. But, Protopopov may have calculated, the Tsar's attitude might be changed by the outbreak of a revolution. That would need troops for its suppression and it might become apparent to the Tsar that the armies could not face in two directions at the same time. He might conclude that it was more important for the armies to face inward than outward, and in those circumstances he might be induced to make peace with Germany.

This, perhaps, was a farfetched theory. However true or false, it was widely believed at the beginning of 1917. The Tsar's government, and so the Tsar himself, could therefore count upon hardly an atom of support from Russian patriots. Nor, of course, could the Tsar count upon the support of the disillusioned and the war-weary when his every other utterance was devoted to the need for continuing the war to an ultimate conclusion. Thus, in the eyes of the patriots who longed for great victories in 1917, the Tsar appeared as a danger and, at least by association, as a traitor. But in the eyes of those who wanted peace at any price, he appeared as an obstacle and a slave driver. The former looked for salvation to the Duma and the latter looked for it to Lenin, who was preaching peace from Geneva.

The Tsar and the Tsaritsa had long been warned of the approaching catastrophe. Before Rasputin's murder much of the advice they received was directed toward the elimination of Rasputin's influence. The Tsar's mother had joined in this and so had several other members of the imperial family but the only result had been to increase the degree of estrangement between them and the Tsaritsa, who even believed that the Grand Duke Paul's grave illness in 1916 was due to his having spoken against Rasputin. The Tsaritsa's sister, the Grand Duchess Elisabeth, had come from Moscow to beg for the banishment of Rasputin, but all that she had received was a sharp reminder of the time of the next train back to Moscow.

The results of these endeavors had become widely known in Petrograd and their frustration had led people more and more to direct their hostility against the Tsaritsa herself. She knew about this largely through the gossip-collecting agency of Madame Vyrubova and she even knew that plots for her removal to a nunnery were being discussed, but she firmly believed that people hated her because she was right and good and strong and they were wrong and evil and jealous.

After Rasputin's death these feelings of hostility were intensified and more directly canalized against the Tsaritsa. Talk of "revolution from above" increased. People almost openly discussed the question of whether it would be necessary to kill the Tsaritsa and the Tsar or merely the Tsaritsa. This too was known to the Tsaritsa and to the Tsar. He had an intense interest in Russian history and he can hardly have failed to appreciate the part which palace revolutions had played in it. Nevertheless, he and the Tsaritsa correctly judged that a palace revolution was not imminent. How they judged the prospects of another and far more radical kind of revolution is another question, but of this too there was no shortage of warnings. Rodzianko, Prince Lvov, and many other representatives of the

Duma, the *Zemstva,* and the town councils constantly urged the Tsar to deal with the situation by the introduction of constitutional measures and by the appointment of what they described as a "responsible government." They all had a touching faith in the efficacy of Western liberalism. But the Tsar and the Tsaritsa had not.

The British ambassador, Sir George Buchanan, who was closely in touch with the currents of liberal opinion in Petrograd, had often hinted to the Tsar that his future depended not upon resisting but upon harnessing those liberal currents. In January 1917 he became more outspoken. He went to the Tsar in the Alexander Palace at Tsarskoe Selo and frankly warned him that the Tsaritsa's entourage had far too much influence over ministerial appointments, and that Protopopov, now the key man in the government, was pro-German and a dangerous traitor. He urged the Tsar to dismiss the government and to appoint one acceptable in the eyes of the Duma. He concluded by warning the Tsar that he was walking straight toward an abyss.

On this occasion the Tsar did not receive Sir George Buchanan informally in his study as he usually did. He received him ceremoniously in the audience chamber. He listened attentively and at the end he thanked the ambassador, but Sir George Buchanan understood perfectly that his advice had fallen upon deaf ears. This can hardly have mattered, for in that audience chamber neither the speaker nor the listener was even faintly aware of the real forces which Russia was now generating. Nor, for that matter, were Rodzianko, Prince Lvov, and the others any more aware.

Over a year earlier, the Tsar had received a much more important and a much more relevant piece of advice. He had received it not from the Duma, not from the *Zemstva,* and not from the British ambassador. He had received it through the Tsaritsa from Rasputin. Toward the end of October 1915 she had written to him of what "Our Friend" had told her on the previous evening. "Now another subject," she had written, "worries him very much and he spoke scarcely about anything else for two hours. It is that you must give an order that waggons with flour, butter and sugar should be obliged to pass. He saw the whole thing in the night like a vision, all the towns, railway lines etc. its difficult to give over fr. his words, but he says it is very serious and that then we shall have no strikes. Only for such an organisation somebody ought to be sent from you. He wishes me to speak to you about all this very earnestly, severely even.... He would propose 3 days no other trains should go except those with flour, butter and sugar—its even more necessary than meat or ammunition just now." [6] Almost exactly a month later, the Tsaritsa had looked at her children and had written, "with anguish I think of their future—so unknown!" [7] It was as well that she saw that future less clearly than Rasputin did.

But now in January 1917, the future of those children was nearer. Rasputin was dead but pressure from the liberals was increasing. Fear and frustration were spreading among the upper classes and in the imperial family itself. Hunger and unemployment were growing among the workers, and especially in Petrograd. The railways were not functioning well and food supplies were not getting through to the towns. In the streets and on the railways cataclysmic events were in the making.

Already the Tsar was a broken man. He had surrendered himself to his fate, he had surrendered his judgment to that of his wife, he had surrendered too much. His face had grown thin and drawn and it was covered with wrinkles. His formerly velvety eyes had faded and seemed unable to concentrate upon any single object, but only to wander aimlessly. A forced and sad smile was often on his lips but there was no longer any joy or hope in his expression. He found it more and more difficult to say unpleasant things or to consider unpleasant situations.

The Tsaritsa still dreamed of future glory. She prayed fervently and almost incessantly. She cried terribly and frequently. Whenever she could she went to the hospital to dress wounds, to hold instruments for the surgeons, or to sit beside the dying. She had moments of bleakest depression but generally her spirit and her conviction of rightness were undaunted and unquenchable. She suffered appallingly. She slept poorly and seldom before three or four in the morning. Repeatedly she took and recorded her temperature. Hardly ever was it normal. Almost every other day she complained of her heart. Her teeth were decaying. Headaches plagued her.

The Tsar and the Tsaritsa could hardly bear to be apart but since the outbreak of war and especially since the Tsar's assumption of the supreme command in September 1915, they had been constantly apart. The Tsar was generally at Mohilev and the Tsaritsa was generally at the Alexander Palace in Tsarskoe Selo. Occasionally she visited him at the headquarters and more often he came for a few days to Tsarskoe Selo, but now, after the murder of Rasputin, he stayed there for several weeks. Some people believed that he had been greatly impressed by Sir George Buchanan's advice and that he was contemplating a radical change in the government. That, however, was hardly likely while he was with the Tsaritsa, and a grand duke even told the British ambassador that if he had been Russian he would have been sent to Siberia for saying what he had said. For less plain speaking, indeed, the Grand Duke Nicholas Michaelovitch was exiled to his estates.

In the event, the only important change made in the government was the dismissal of Trepov, who had tried so hard and so strangely to master Rasputin. In his place, Prince Golitzin was appointed as President of the Council. Protopopov remained as Minister of the Interior. Everyone knew that the situation in Petrograd was growing tense but no one seemed to expect a revolution in the immediate future. Indeed, the absurd thing about revolutions is that they never seem to be expected— even by the revolutionaries. Nevertheless, it was obvious even to the outsider that the Tsar and the Tsaritsa were, as one such outsider put it, "riding for a fall." Nor were there many who regretted the prospect. "It seems as certain as anything can be,"

British General Sir Henry Wilson recorded during his visit to Russia for the allied conference in Petrograd, "that the Emperor and Empress are riding for a fall. Everyone—officers, merchants, ladies—talk openly of the absolute necessity of doing away with them." [8] Officially, General Wilson was not much concerned. He had inspected the Russian army at the front and he had been profoundly impressed by it. "The *civiles* are anxious about the internal state," he wrote. "I am not, as, even if the Tsar and the Tsarina are assassinated, it will not make for a separate peace." [9]

Personally, the general was much affected by the prospect which he misjudged so badly. He describes how, at Tsarskoe Selo, after dining with the Tsar, he was "taken down a long passage to the Empress's own boudoir—a room full of pictures and bric-à-brac and flowers, and a large gallery. She was very pleasant and nice to me," he wrote. "I reminded her of our tennis parties in the old days, 36 years ago, at Darmstadt, where I said I used to play tennis with her and her sisters. She was so delighted with the reminiscences, and remembered some of the names I had forgotten. After this it was easy. She said her lot was harder than most people's because she had relations and friends in England, Russia and Germany. She told me of her experiences, and her eyes filled with tears. She has a beautiful face, but very, very sad. She is tall and graceful, divides her hair simply at one side, and it is done up at the back. The hair is powdered with grey. When I said I was going to leave her, as she must be tired of seeing strangers and making conversation, she nearly laughed and kept me on for a little while. What a tragedy there is in that life." [10] But General Wilson knew only a fraction of her tragedy. Undoubtedly, the Tsaritsa did not speak to him of Rasputin's death or of her son's health.

The general was also sorry for the Tsar. He was "astonished to find much more character in his face than I had imagined, and quite a twinkle in his eye...." But he added, "What a murderous pity that the Emperor is so weak and so under the Empress's thumb, for, according to all the accounts I get, he

and the Empress are heading straight for ruin." [11] Here, it is
strange to reflect, was the sympathy of one who was to be
assassinated for two who were to be murdered.

On February 27, 1917, the Duma resumed its sittings. The
initial proceedings passed off very quietly. Sir George Buchanan
thought that it would be a good time to go away for a holiday
in Finland and he did so. On March 7th the Tsar left Tsarskoe
Selo to return to Mohilev where his presence was urgently
demanded by the chief of staff, General Alexeiev. The weather
was sunny and frosty. On the journey the Tsar "read, was bored
and rested." [12] On the next day there were stormy scenes in the
Duma when the government was accused of having taken inadequate measures to provision Petrograd. Queues of people
were standing outside the bread shops and most of them were
getting no bread. On that day there was some looting of the
shops and in the evening a patrol of Cossacks galloped down
the Nevski to disperse the crowd. Also on the same day, March
8th, the Tsar heard from Tsarskoe Selo that two of his children,
the Grand Duchess Olga and the Tsarevitch, had developed
measles.

On March 9th there was renewed agitation in the streets of
Petrograd, and once again Cossack mounted patrols appeared.
The crowd, though hungry, was good-humored and readily
gave ground to the Cossacks. They even cheered them and
many Cossacks were seen to join in friendly conversation with
the people. Toward the police, however, the crowds showed
the utmost hostility. On that day the Tsar heard that another
of his children, the Grand Duchess Tatiana, had got measles,
and he wrote a rather strange letter to the Tsaritsa. He observed
that the rooms in the Alexander Palace would have to be fumi-
gated. He supposed that Peterhof would be an unsuitable residence. He suggested a move to the Crimea after Easter. He
thought it would be good for the Tsarevitch's health.

On March 10th what amounted to a general strike was declared in Petrograd. Crowds again surged up and down the
streets and the demonstration began to assume a more organized

kind of appearance. The Minister of War, General Belaiev, sent a telegram to Mohilev saying that strikes had broken out but giving an assurance that order would be quickly and easily restored. The Tsar wrote to the Tsaritsa thanking God that the attacks of measles were not producing complications but saying that railway connections had been dislocated by snow and that the armies at the front were threatened by famine within three or four days.

On March 11th the military governor of Petrograd, General Habalov, posted up notices all over the town warning strikers that they would be sent to the front if they persisted and warning everybody that the troops and police had orders to disperse all crowds. These warnings were completely ignored. The crowds grew larger and in the course of the day some hundreds of demonstrators were killed in clashes with the troops. In the afternoon a company of the Pavlovsk Regiment mutinied when ordered to fire on the crowd. It was quickly disarmed and by evening something like order had apparently been restored. But the crowds who had initially demanded bread were now demanding the overthrow of the government. General Belaiev telegraphed to Mohilev reporting that some troops had defected but saying that the situation was again wholly in hand. General Habalov, on the other hand, sent more alarming reports and asked for reinforcements. The President of the Duma, Rodzianko, warned the Tsar that the situation could be saved only by concessions to the people, the dismissal of the government, and the appointment of one responsible to the Duma. The Tsar hoped that General Habalov would be able to stop these "street disorders" and he told the Tsaritsa that "clear and definite instructions" must be given by Protopopov.[13] But Rodzianko did not send his telegram only to the Tsar. He sent copies of it together with an appeal for support to the commanders at the front. The Tsar appointed General Ivanov, who had so greatly distinguished himself earlier in the war, to proceed with the suppression of the disorders and he decided himself to leave the front and to return within a day or two to Tsarskoe Selo. He telegraphed to the Tsaritsa: "Am leaving the day after tomorrow. Have finished here with all important questions. Sleep well. May God bless you all!" [14] But the Tsaritsa was not unduly disturbed by the situation. "This is a hooligan movement," she had written to the Tsar on the previous day. "Boys and girls run about and yell that they have no bread simply in order to create a disturbance—and workers who prevent others from working. If the weather had been really cold, they would probably have stayed at home." [15] On the next day she was still optimistic. "All adore you and only want bread," she told the Tsar.[16]

On March 12th, in Petrograd, the Preobrazhenski Regiment was ordered to fire upon the crowd. It turned and shot its officers. The Volynski Regiment was ordered to disarm the mutineers but instead it followed their example. By midday, twenty-five thousand troops had joined the crowd or, in other words, had gone over to the revolution. The army was making common cause with the people. The revolt was now armed. A military arsenal was stormed and taken. The Law Courts were burned. Prisons were opened. Alcohol flowed in greater quantities than blood. The Tsar's brother, the Grand Duke Michael, telephoned to General Alexeiev from Petrograd and urged him to advise the Tsar to appoint either Rodzianko or Prince Lvov as President of the Council. The existing President of the Council, Prince Golitzin, reported that the government was collapsing and also urged the appointment of Rodzianko or Prince Lvov. In particular, he advised the immediate dismissal of Protopopov. The Tsar replied that no changes could be considered at the moment. General Alexeiev, who on that day had a temperature of 102°, begged him to reconsider this decision. But the Tsar refused.

Meanwhile, crowds of revolutionary troops and others approached the Duma building in Petrograd. They were received by Rodzianko and by Kerensky, the leader of the social revolutionaries in the Duma. Rodzianko assured the visitors that the Duma would not dissolve as it had been ordered to do and that, on the contrary, it intended to overthrow the government.

Kerensky spoke against excesses and arranged for the provision of an armed military guard for the Duma building. The Duma then appointed an executive committee with Rodzianko at its head. It included representatives of all parties except that of the extreme right. Among its members were Kerensky and another socialist, Cheidze, who was leader of the Social Democrats.

The Tsar and the Tsar's government had now been overridden by the Duma's Provisional Government but the Provisional Government, consisting of liberals, conservatives, socialists, moderates, and progressivists, was already in danger. At the very moment of its birth, and in the same Duma building, the Executive Committee of the Council of Workmen's and Soldiers' Delegates also assembled. This was not a "representative" body. It consisted of Bolsheviks. In the evening, Protopopov surrendered to the Duma Provisional Government and was imprisoned. At one o'clock in the morning on March 13th, the Tsar boarded the imperial train at Mohilev. A few hours later it left for Tsarskoe Selo. From Viazma the Tsar telegraphed to the Tsaritsa, "Left this morning at 5 o'clock. In thought I am always with you. Wonderful weather. I hope that you are feeling well and are calm. Many troops have been sent from the front. Heartiest greetings." [17] Later on the same day he telegraphed again, this time from Lichoslavl, saying, "Thanks for news. Am glad that all is well with you. Hope to be home tomorrow morning. Embrace you and the children. God guard you." [18]

But these messages did not get through to the Tsaritsa. Generally her telegrams to the Tsar were answered by him within two hours. Now she had heard nothing from him for forty-eight hours. Clearly something had gone wrong and it was left to the Tsaritsa's distracted imagination to guess what it might be. Already her own plight in the Alexander Palace was sufficient to nullify any optimistic interpretation of the Tsar's silence which might have occurred to her. On the evening of March 12th, Rodzianko—"fat Rodzianko" whom the Tsaritsa hated so bitterly—had telephoned from the Duma building in Petrograd to Count Benckendorff in the Alexander Palace at Tsarskoe Selo. He had advised the Tsaritsa to take her children and leave immediately for a more remote area.

This was better advice than she would have got from the Tsar even if his messages had reached her. But there was a fatal hesitation. Certainly the Tsaritsa's position was a difficult one. Her children were going down one by one with measles. There were no complications but the illnesses were serious. A long journey on the disorganized railways in the Russian winter was hardly an encouraging prospect and especially so in the case of the Tsarevitch. For him any ailment was a serious thing. Even so the Tsaritsa seems to have decided to leave. At any rate she gave orders on the morning of March 13th for the packing to be done.

By that time, however, it was too late. The imperial train could no longer be extricated from its siding in Petrograd. Once more, and for the last time, the Tsaritsa had failed to heed a warning. On the evening of March 13th the garrison at Tsarskoe Selo joined the revolution and opened the local prison. As darkness fell, the sound of shooting could clearly be heard from within the Alexander Palace. The Tsaritsa tried to reassure her children by telling them that what they heard was due to routine military maneuvers. But she herself, perhaps for the first time in her life, began to grasp what the real situation was. Both the water and electricity supplies to the palace were cut off and an attack upon it by revolutionary troops and a drunken mob seemed to be imminent.

There were hardly any means of defending the palace and the guard was preparing to make the most of what it had got. In the chill of the night the Tsaritsa and her daughter, the Grand Duchess Marie, came out to see the men. The Tsaritsa urged them to avoid bloodshed and then withdrew to await what she may well have expected to be the end. She sat in her room beneath a huge portrait of Marie Antoinette.

The night was an anxious one. A resolute attack by the

revolutionary troops outside would easily have succeeded. The palace could at any moment have been opened to a crowd of jailbirds and drunken hooligans. But the revolutionary troops too had been drinking heavily. It seemed to them that the palace defenses were formidable and they could scarcely believe that "bloody Nicholas" would have left his wife and children without effective protection. That, however, was precisely what he had done. There was a great deal of shouting and posturing. There was some shooting but there was no attack and in the more sober light of the dawn the forces of the revolution in Tsarskoe Selo decided to approach their object from farther away. They uprooted themselves and set off to join their comrades in Petrograd.

What they did there and, indeed, most of what was happening in Petrograd was unknown to the Tsaritsa. There was still a telephone connection with the Winter Palace in the capital but the reports from it naturally referred only to what was happening in the immediate vicinity. The Tsaritsa was as unaware of the course of the revolution as she had been of its cause, but at least the immediate threat to her life and to the lives of her children had been relieved. Not knowing what to think, she turned once more to the strenuous task of nursing four sick children and the devoted Anna Vyrubova, who had also got measles and, as was natural to her, was feeling extremely sorry for herself. On top of this, the Grand Duchess Marie now developed measles and pneumonia, from which she was presently almost to die. Her younger sister, the Grand Duchess Anastasia, was suffering badly from a particularly virulent attack of measles.

Meanwhile, in Petrograd, the revolution was rushing toward its first great and already inevitable climax. On March 13th the Admiralty building surrendered and the last remnant of the Tsar's government collapsed. Only three members of it, indeed, were still at liberty. More and more soldiers fraternized with the people and there was no longer any prospect whatever of saving the monarchy by military action. Ten thousand well-armed, vigorously led, and completely loyal troops might have saved the situation but such a body of men did not appear to exist, and even if it did no one seemed to have the will to find it, let alone to lead it into action. The Tsaritsa was marooned at Tsarskoe Selo and the Tsar had disappeared in a train. No one was prepared to shed any blood for either of them. Even so there were many who wished to preserve the monarchy. The best means of doing that seemed to be the immediate abdication of Nicholas II in favor of his son. That was the course which the head of the Duma Committee, Rodzianko, now favored and advocated. Already the soldiers of the army had played a decisive part in the revolution. Now it was the turn of the generals.

The Tsar, it will be remembered, had left Mohilev for Tsarskoe Selo early on the morning of March 13th. The train journey, which is among the most remarkable recorded in history, started under normal conditions. At the stations dignitaries were drawn up in their usual obsequious ranks and the Tsar, of course, seemed to be quite unconcerned. Gradually, however, it became apparent that the revolution had exerted a grip on the railways. Long before the train reached its destination it stopped and the Tsar was told that the line was cut. He was told that it was impossible to reach Tsarskoe Selo. He decided to head for Pskov where General Russky, the commander of the Northern front, had his headquarters. What the Tsar's plan was or whether he had a plan at all was uncertain.

Several of his suite showed alarm. The Tsar of Russia could no longer decide the destination of his own train but the Tsar of Russia, outwardly at least, showed not only no sign of alarm but no sign of any concern whatsoever. His behavior was exactly as usual. He continued to engage his suite in inconsequential conversation, he ate his meals as usual, and he slept well. If anything, he seemed to be in better form than usual.

When General Russky heard that the Tsar was approaching

his headquarters at Pskov he immediately got into touch with General Alexeiev at Mohilev and demanded that the opinions of the army commanders should be sounded and communicated to him at Pskov before the Tsar's arrival there. General Loukhomsky, the quartermaster general at Mohilev, undertook this delicate task and the issue which he put to the commanders boiled down in substance to the question: Do you or do you not favor the abdication of the Tsar? Clearly both General Loukhomsky and General Alexeiev did. Presently General Ebert telephoned from the Eastern front saying that his attitude would be conditioned by what Generals Brussilov and Russky thought. General Brussilov sent a telegram favoring abdication. General Loukhomsky then told General Ebert of this and added that General Russky was of the same opinion. General Ebert cast his vote for abdication. The Grand Duke Nicholas, who addressed his message directly to the Tsar but sent a copy to Mohilev, said that abdication was the only solution. General Sarkarov from the Rumanian front expressed strong condemnation of the Duma but admitted that he could see no alternative to abdication. General Alexeiev sent all this information to General Russky at Pskov, adding his own advice to the effect that the Tsar's abdication was essential. Such was the attitude of the generals in whose company the Tsar had so much delighted. Apart from General Sarkarov, almost the only one who really regretted the situation was the Englishman at Mohilev, General Sir John Hanbury Williams, who could not smile at what seemed to him to be shabby conduct. Thus, as the soldiers had already thrown in their lot with the people, so now the generals threw in their lot with Rodzianko and his Duma Committee.

Rodzianko and his Duma Committee had already dispatched two delegates, Gutchkov and Schoulguin, to Pskov with instructions to explain the situation to the Tsar and to secure his abdication. When the Tsar arrived there on the evening of March 14th he was therefore confronted with a carefully prepared situation which, even if he had remotely anticipated it, he could not possibly have changed.

But Nicholas II not only had not anticipated the situation, he was quite unable to understand it when he was confronted with it. Abdication, the last act of Nicholas II as Tsar, was an almost incredible revelation of his failure to come to grips with facts and of his reluctance even to think about unpleasant things.

The next day the Tsar had to take his decision alone. He could not consult the Tsaritsa, and without the Tsaritsa, in a situation like this he was really nothing. He offered no resistance to the idea of abdication. Indeed, even before the arrival of the Duma delegates, Nicholas had shown General Russky his readiness to abdicate and had handed over a signed document to that effect. In fact he seemed to treat the whole question of surrendering the imperial crown of all the Russias as though he were handing over a company of guards to their commander after an inspection. Never before had the Tsar's lifelong training in the precept that it is not done to show one's feelings been more clearly exemplified and never before had the reasons for his personal failure as a sovereign been more strikingly demonstrated. At the end, as throughout his reign, Nicholas II allowed himself to be carried along by the force of circumstances and by the will of stronger characters than his own. Accordingly, there was no difficulty in preparing a manifesto in which the Tsar renounced the throne in favor of his son, the Tsarevitch Alexis.

When the two Duma delegates arrived, some of the implications of what he was doing gradually dawned upon him. He remarked to Gutchkov that he thought of retiring to the Crimea and living there with his family. He asked whether that would be satisfactory to the new government. Gutchkov told him that it would not and explained that the ex-Tsar would have to reside in exile abroad. Such an idea had not occurred to the man who was signing away his crown. He paused. Then he asked where the new Tsar would live. In Russia, he was told. It was now clear to Nicholas that abdication in favor of his son would mean separation from his son. He began to think about the boy's health. He began to reconsider or, to be more precise, to consider his position. He withdrew and sought the advice of his physician, Feodorov, the same Feodorov who had contemplated a drastic remedy for the Tsarevitch's illness at Spala in 1912.

The Tsar put a number of questions to Feodorov about the nature of the Tsarevitch's hemophilia. It was evident that up to this moment he had never been able to bring himself to the point of any conclusion on that subject. Feodorov explained to him that the Tsarevitch suffered incurably from the disease, that he might live for many years or only a few days but that in either case his life would always be precariously balanced as upon a knife edge. In that knowledge the Tsar could no longer bear the prospect of separation from his son. He changed the manifesto and abdicated in favor of his brother, the Grand Duke Michael.

Thus, Nicholas II signed away the crown which he had so long hoped and so hopelessly striven to transmit intact to his son, and at the same time disinherited that son. The tragic irony of that act was that, ever since 1904, the Tsar had convinced himself that his duty and his object, in view of the fragile health of his heir, was to create conditions in which Alexis could reign without undue exertion. Now, and also because of that fragile health, he ensured that his son would never reign at all. But the irony was greater than that, for there was, in effect, no Russian crown left to sign away.

In a telegram to the Tsaritsa from Pskov, sent on the day of his abdication, the Tsar made no reference to that act. He hoped that "everybody's health is better and that we shall soon see each other." [19] He left it to others to break the news to his wife that she was no longer Tsaritsa. Only in his diary did he offer an explanation of his action and even an uncharacteristic complaint about the cause of it. Thirty messages had been received from army commanders. "The main point is," the Tsar wrote, "that for the sake of saving Russia and keeping the army in the field, it is necessary to decide on this step. I agreed. ... Left Pskov at one in the morning. All around me I see treason, cowardice and deceit." [20]

VI

Humiliation

THE abdication of Nicholas II, like the murder of Rasputin, was a complete fiasco. It did not save the monarchy, it did not check the revolution, it did not keep the armies in the field, and it did not save the Tsar. It did not even save his chilren. The Tsar's brother and designated successor never reigned. When he heard that the abdication was in his favor, the Grand Duke Michael renounced his claim until a decision should be reached by the representatives of the people. The end of Nicholas II's reign was the end of the Russian monarchy, for the collapse was due not only to the personal failure of the monarch but also to the institutional failure of the monarchy. Alexander II, who had striven to reform the regime, had succeeded only in releasing a flood of revolutionary violence of which he himself had been the victim. Alexander III had repressed the wave of violence but only at the price of ignoring the necessity for reform. Nicholas II had offered neither reform nor effective repression. There had been a failure in the monarch but there was also a failure in the monarchy and the two had come together in the greatest and most terrible war which Russia had ever fought.

Throughout his reign, Nicholas II had been mercilessly tossed by the waves of forces which were incomprehensible to him. His vague ideas of duty, autocracy, and tradition were wholly irrelevant. His rather clearer idea of transmitting an inheritance to his son was pathetic. The only realism in his outlook was his constant sense of approaching doom. Without the Tsaritsa he would have been incapable of the blunders for which she was responsible, but without the Tsaritsa he could hardly have carried on at all. Nor, of course, did the Tsaritsa's dream of glory have any more relevance than the Tsar's lesser ideas. It was not only that Nicholas II was psychologically incapable of being the kind of sovereign she envisaged but that the vision itself had no real meaning. The late nineteenth and early twentieth century was not the golden age of mysticism. It was, as the Tsaritsa herself occasionally recognized and always deplored, the heydey of rational materialism.

Thus, in March 1917, the Tsar and the Tsaritsa had to face not only the humiliation of failure but the greater one of irrelevance. In a day, and without a shot being fired, they became political nonentities and, as such, it might have been expected that they would disappear into the mist of an obscure retirement.

If the revolution had been purely political, no doubt that is what would have happened. But the revolution, of course, was not purely political: it was also emotional and, from the German point of view, it was strategic. Moreover, the political significance, even of an autocrat, is less important than his symbolic significance. During his reign Nicholas had been the symbol of the existing order—its coat of arms. After his abdication he became the symbol of what was being destroyed—the whipping boy of Russian history. After the abdication, Nicholas and his family therefore continued to be significant people not only as outrageous symbols but as potential bargaining counters between the various forces of revolution and between Germany and Russia. Their fate was no longer influenced to the slightest extent by their own actions or attitudes, and here was the ultimate humiliation. From kings they had become pawns.

This transformation, seemingly so dramatic, was, however, in the case of Nicholas himself, more apparent than real. He had always regarded himself as the pawn of fate and he had always been the prisoner of superior forces whether of character or of circumstance. Indeed, his whole outlook and his whole life was the ideal preparation and the perfect qualification for physical imprisonment. Moreover, it is prison that places the highest value upon an ability to concentrate upon the inconsequential and the trivial. But, for the Tsaritsa, the transformation was a real and devastating one. Her positive and strong character had led her to believe that she was the mistress of circumstances and her mystical faith had convinced her that she could change them. Her fall was immeasurably greater than the Tsar's. But their agony was equal—hers because of what had happened, and his because of what had happened to her.

Even this was less than half of the approaching tragedy, for in the inexorable grip of circumstances and of fate there were also caught the five devoted children of the Tsar and the Tsaritsa. The eldest of them, the Grand Duchess Olga, was now twenty-one. She had blond hair and beautiful blue eyes and though her manners were brusque she was simple, sincere, and kindhearted. She was modest and paid little attention to her appearance, but she had a developed musical and artistic talent. She painted nicely, played the piano well, and sang soprano. The Grand Duchess Olga was fond of reading and had an appreciation of poetry. She spoke English well and German badly and, in addition to Russian, like her sisters and her brother, she spoke French. She was especially devoted to her father whom in many respects she resembled. She had no immediate plans for marriage and the Rumanian Prince Carol, who had been considered as a prospective husband, did not appeal to her. During the war she had devoted herself as her mother had done to nursing.

The Grand Duchess Tatiana, now nineteen years old, was entirely different. In appearance and in manner she strongly resembled her mother to whom she was devoted. She was slender, tall, and elegant. Her eyes were dark gray and her complexion was darker than her elder sister's. She played the piano very competently but without much feeling and in other respects was less cultivated than the Grand Duchess Olga. Her manner was reserved and haughty and she had strong opinions which mingled with a dedicated sense of duty. Her elder sister usually deferred to her judgment and it was easy to see that the Grand Duchess Tatiana was an imperial personage. Like her mother at the same age, her youth was belied by her appearance and her demeanor. Undoubtedly she was the Tsaritsa's favorite daughter.

The Grand Duchess Marie was seventeen at the time of the abdication. She was strikingly attractive, had light gray eyes, light brown hair, and a beautiful face. She was a powerfully built girl of great strength and the Tsarevitch's English tutor, Mr. Gibbs, remembered that she could easily lift him into the air. The Grand Duchess Marie was a considerable artist and was especially fond of pencil drawings. She was modest and simple in her tastes and tended distinctly to be lazy. She was devoted to small children. She had an excellent memory for details and she always seemed to remember the names of the wives, the numbers of children, and the amount of land belonging to the peasant soldiers to whom she spoke.

The youngest daughter, the Grand Duchess Anastasia, was fifteen. She was shorter than her sisters and inclined to be fat. She was the least graceful member of the family and was, of course, at the least graceful age. She had beautiful gray eyes and light brown hair which lay flat on her forehead. Physically she was somewhat overdeveloped for her age, but mentally she was underdeveloped and in her general education she was distinctly backward. But the Grand Duchess Anastasia had a pronounced talent. She was a born mimic and had an unfailing ability in spotting the humorous aspects of those she represented. She made everyone laugh, but she seldom laughed herself.

The Tsarevitch Alexis was twelve years old and was the idol of the family. He was tall for his age but had the terrible thinness of suffering and illness. He had a kind heart and an especially developed sympathy for the sufferings of others. He was devoted to animals. The Tsarevitch had a lively and original mind but he was not fond of books or of lessons. Latterly he wrote a diary with a good deal of grumbling but in all academic

pursuits he was backward and his tuition was greatly and frequently disrupted by his illness. He had to be trained to curb
his high spirits, but his natural vigor resulted in an almost
constant series of minor accidents which had grave consequences. His life was an agony of suffering and even when he
was supposedly well he often had a stiff arm or a painful knee.
If he spent a completely peaceful night without waking up, it
was usually a subject of gratified family comment. He had a
strong character, always knew his own mind, and was difficult
to control. His father was the only person whom he always
obeyed, and the Tsaritsa his mother could not help spoiling
him. He once remarked of a photograph of himself and a dog
that the dog looked the more intelligent. Some believe that
the boy had looked upon Rasputin with distaste.

The imperial children had no intimate friends outside their
immediate family circle. Their tastes and their social life were
simple and circumscribed. The bond of affection which united
them and bound them to their parents was as strong as the
bond which united their parents with each other and with
them. Beyond that they never seemed to look. The seven devoted members of the imperial family were affectionately self-
sufficient. They were all borne up by strong religious faith and
all that they feared on earth was separation from each other.

When the Tsar had completed his act of abdication at Pskov,
he was advised that he might return to Mohilev to take leave
of the troops and hand over the supreme command. That,
accordingly, was the direction in which he was traveling when
he left Pskov at one in the morning with a heavy heart. It was
the morning of March 16th. He talked to his companions about
the events of the previous day and he read "much about Julius
Caesar." [1] Back at Tsarskoe Selo the Tsaritsa still had no news
of what was happening. On March 14th, the day on which
she had expected him to arrive, she heard that his train had
been delayed and was now approaching by a different route.
She began to fear that her husband might have been murdered,

which indeed was hardly an unlikely possibility. At the same time the unhappy Tsaritsa had to face the prospect that the Alexander Palace might at any moment be stormed by the mob or by revolutionary troops. In addition, her daughter, the Grand Duchess Marie, was now dangerously ill with a simultaneous attack of measles and pneumonia. Nor could the Tsaritsa know whether measles would prove to be within or beyond the strength of her son's resistance. No longer could she turn to Rasputin in whose power of healing she had had such an absolute faith. She could only remember the *Staretz*'s prophecy that the life of her adored son depended upon his own.

By any standard, the Tsaritsa's position was unenviable. By her own, it was desperate, but at this time she found and displayed resources of courage and of calm which few had previously suspected were within her power. She nursed her children and inspired those around her with some sort of faith which enabled them to carry on. At last it became known in Tsarskoe Selo that the Tsar had abdicated. The Tsaritsa could not believe it but when the Grand Duke Paul came and confirmed the news, she recognized that her husband's reign had been interrupted. Even then she could not register the real meaning of what had happened. "The people will change their minds," she told the Grand Duke. "They will call Alexis to the throne and all will be well." [2] When Alexis himself was told that his father had abdicated and that he was no longer the heir to the throne, he wondered who then would be Tsar, for he simply could not imagine Russia without a Tsar. Nor could the Tsaritsa. Wandering from one idea to another, she wrote to Nicholas on the day after his abdication, "Oh my hero . . . I swear by my life that we shall see you again on the throne raised again by your people and army to the glory of your reign." [3] But behind this assurance there was, of course, no more substance than there had been behind her plan of the day before to send an airplane to rescue the Tsar from the mousetrap in which he had been caught.

Meanwhile, the Tsar had come to the end of his extraordinary train journey, in the course of which and at a cost of fewer than a thousand lives, he had been cast aside, the monarchy had been destroyed, and an epoch had been ended. He was back at Mohilev simply as "Colonel Romanov"—back at Mohilev, which he had left a few days earlier as Tsar of all the Russias and Supreme Commander of all the armies. There he was joined by his mother, who hastened from Kiev to comfort her stricken son, but whether Nicholas was in need of comfort or not, he gave no outward sign whatsoever of the staggering transformation which had occurred in his life. He paid no attention to the various suggestions made to him about his possible escape. He rejected the offers of protection and assistance made to him by the heads of the allied military missions at Mohilev. All he wished was to be reunited with his family at Tsarskoe Selo and all he did was to await with absolute calm his orders from the revolutionary government.

The revolution had triumphed absolutely. No one stood forth for the Tsar or for any other Tsar. The newspapers were full of abuse for the imperial family. Stories about Rasputin, suggestions that the Tsaritsa was pro-German, and accusations that the Tsar had been preparing a separate peace with her German cousin filled column after column and those who could read, read avidly. But if it was clear that the revolution had triumphed, it was not clear what sort of revolution it was. The Provisional Government, led by Prince Lvov, was the constitutional successor of the monarchy. It sprang from the imperial Duma and it had, as his final official act, been recognized by the Tsar. Its policy was to summon a constituent assembly and to devise a new Russian constitution. Meanwhile, the war was to be continued until final victory had been won. Russia was to be a good deal more liberal and perhaps a little socialist, but she was still to be Russia in her basic social system and in her foreign policy.

However, the Provisional Government had a rival—the Committee of Workers' and Soldiers' Delegates which, like the Provisional Government, was entrenched in the Duma building from where it issued decrees and orders of various kinds. This Committee was the constitutional successor of nothing. It was the real product of revolution and it was the heir of violence. For leadership, it looked across Germany to Switzerland, where Lenin was now approaching the end of his exile, and across the Atlantic to Canada, from where Trotsky was preparing to come home. The policy of the Committee was to achieve the Bolshevik revolution not merely in Russia but in the world. The workers everywhere were to unite and overthrow their masters and oppressors. War between nations was to end. War between classes was to begin. The Bolsheviks stood for the overthrow of society at home and for peace at almost any price abroad.

The Provisional Government either did not or dared not recognize the inevitability of the struggle with the Committee. They, and in particular their leading and most left-wing personality, Alexander Kerensky, thought in terms of conciliation and possibly of coalition. In time they would become the first of the victims of coalition with communism.

In the meantime the Provisional Government held the initiative but it was a qualified initiative, and qualified especially insofar as the fate of the Tsar and his family was concerned. Now more than ever the unfortunate family was caught in the vise of contending forces and circumstances which they could neither understand nor even imagine. On March 20, 1917, the Provisional Government, of which Kerensky was the Minister of Justice, resolved to arrest the Tsar and the Tsaritsa.

Four representatives of the Provisional Government were dispatched to Mohilev where they arrived on March 21st. They told the Tsar of the decision and then entrained him for Tsarskoe Selo. For the last time Nicholas embarked upon the familiar journey. Apart from the absence of officials to greet him at the stopping places, he traveled much as usual, accompanied, as before, by his suite headed by Prince Dolgoruky, the second marshal of his court. Nicholas and his mother had seen each other for the last time.

While this was happening at Mohilev, General Kornilov

arrived at the Alexander Palace in Tsarskoe Selo to arrest the Tsaritsa. He was accompanied by Colonel Kotsebue, who had been appointed commandant of the palace, and by Colonel Kobylinsky, who was to be commandant of the Tsarskoe Selo garrison. Something of the old form was still preserved. General Kornilov was received on his arrival by Count Benckendorff, the grand marshal of the court, and it was through him that an audience with the Tsaritsa was sought. The Tsaritsa was then told of the government's decision and the two colonels were presented to her. She said little but extended her hand to the visitors and they bowed to her. The palace entourage were told that it was only the Tsaritsa who was being arrested and that any of them who wished to leave might do so provided that they made their decision within twenty-four hours. Some availed themselves of this opportunity—among them the personal servant of the Tsarevitch, who not only cleared out, but cleared out with several of his young master's possessions. Even so, there were many brave people who remained steadfastly loyal. Several of them were eventually to pay for their devotion with their lives and, even if this could not be foreseen, the danger of loyalty was already clear, for those who remained were now liable to abuse and insult. Neither rank nor nationality was the mark of loyalty. Among those who elected to stay were Count Benckendorff, two ladies in waiting, Baroness Buxhoeveden and Countess Hendrikova, the court physician, Dr. Botkin, two maids, Maria Tutelberg and Anna Demidova, a number of waiters, footmen, and cooks, and sailor Nagorny, who was the Tsarevitch's attendant, and the Swiss, M. Gilliard, who was his tutor in French. Madame Vyrubova was steadfast and though there were few outside the palace who now wanted to enter it as friends or servants of the imperial family, there was one who did. He was Mr. Gibbs, the Englishman, who was the Tsarevitch's tutor in English. But the palace was now sealed off from the outside world and it was easier to leave than to enter it.

It seems that at this moment the five imperial children might have been allowed to leave and to join their grandmother in the south, but they were all ill or convalescent and, in any case, the idea of separation from their parents was unthinkable to them. Thus the net was closed. It was a net with a complicated mesh.

Both the Tsar and the Tsaritsa were told that they were being arrested in the interests of their own safety and there was, of course, something in this. We have already seen the parlous condition in which the Tsaritsa had been left by the revolution. The palace was virtually without defenses, its guard was unreliable and to a great extent had melted away. On all sides, people were being incited to hatred of their former ruler and the country was already swarming with deserters from the army. But the leaders of the Provisional Government were less well disposed toward the imperial family than some of them have subsequently tried to represent. They knew well enough that revolutions thrive upon symbols of hatred and they knew that revolutionaries have a natural tendency to kick a dog when he is down. Several of them, indeed, had that tendency themselves. Already, the government had proclaimed that there would be an official investigation of the conduct of the Tsar and the Tsaritsa while they were reigning. Perhaps they wished to discover objectively whether the rumors of pro-German tendencies in the Tsaritsa and the Tsar had any foundation, but more probably they wished to demonstrate to the Bolsheviks and other kinds of extremists that they were no respecters of imperial personages.

However that may have been, and whether the Provisional Government was bidding against the extremists or whether it was simply incapable of controlling them, a series of insults and humiliations was now heaped upon the imperial family. And indeed the greatest of these was the claim of the government that the safety of the prisoners depended upon their arrest and upon the protection of the soldiers of the revolution who now stood guard over them.

The train in which the Tsar traveled as a prisoner from

Mohilev arrived at Tsarskoe Selo on the morning of March 22nd. The former sovereign alighted with Prince Dolgoruky and entered a car. As he did so a mass of his servants and courtiers, having removed his monogram from their uniforms, descended from the train and disappeared into the crowd which was looking on. Here, indeed, was "treason, cowardice and deceit." The goose could no longer lay the golden egg but the ruined master was hardly the worse off for being short of his worthless and faithless servants. For the first time in his life the Tsar could be sure that those who still served him did so for honor and not for greed.

At a quarter past eleven the car reached the palace. There it was challenged by Colonel Kotsebue, who demanded to know whom it contained. "Nicholas Romanov," replied the driver. "Let him pass," said the commandant. The Tsar got out and pressed forward with Prince Dolgoruky through a crowd of soldiers. He was dressed in his familiar military uniform, his face was expressionless, he did not speak, and as he advanced he saluted mechanically. The Prince at his side was in tears. Nicholas went straight upstairs to join his wife and there, perhaps for the first and certainly for the last time in his life, he broke down and cried.

VII

Captivity

NICHOLAS II and Alexandra Feodorovna were now together in adversity and in captivity. They had all of every day to reflect upon the wreck of their reign and it would hardly have been surprising if their marriage as well had now gone on the rocks. The Tsar, after all, had virtually delegated his sovereign functions to his wife and on countless occasions he had deferred to her wish against his own better judgment. Then, while he was away with the armies, the regime had foundered and he had been presented with no alternative to abdication. He might well have turned to the Tsaritsa and blamed her for the failure. Many who had lost much less than he did precisely that.

The Tsaritsa, on the other hand, had firmly believed that all would be well if only the Tsar could be strong and domineering. Over and over again she had seen his weakness and his indecisiveness, and at last he had left her almost unprotected at a critical moment and, without even telling her, had abdicated for himself and her son. She would have been no more than human if she had now turned upon her husband and accused him of betrayal.

Nor was that the full extent of the stress. Nicholas had pleaded desperately for the hand of the Princess Alix. For him, she had changed her religion and left her country. For him, she had come to Russia—the Russia of the last of the Romanovs. Then Nicholas himself had sacrificed much of the pleasure of his earlier life for the sake of the wife he loved so much. He had parted company with many of his friends and some of his relations because she did not like them. He had patiently submitted to her hysterical exhortations and sympathetically endured her almost continuous succession of ailments. She had given him a son who, through her own heredity, was fatally diseased.

Such considerations, however, did not enter into the thoughts of the couple. There was no recrimination between them. Together they had ascended the throne and together they descended from it. They were united in captivity as they had been in power and eventually they were to be united in death as they had been in life. But despite the strength of the bond between them they showed quite different reactions to the days of their persecution.

Alexandra had a blind faith in the goodness of simple men and even the insults of common soldiers did nothing to dim it. She was always convinced that behind the façade of revolutionary leaders, there stood millions of loyal peasants ready to throw themselves at the feet of their Tsar and at her own. She did not lose faith in her dream of future glory—in her conviction that the people would change their minds. Rebuffs from common and simple people she could bear stoically because she did not believe in their reality, but toward the revolutionary leaders or their representatives she was always hostile in intention, and in manner cold, imperious, and haughty. To no one did she ever behave as anything less than a Tsaritsa and anyone of any importance who treated her as less than that was intolerable to her. The rest of her life was a horrible blend of hope and humiliation.

Nicholas could no longer be humiliated. Having never really felt himself to be a Tsar, he scarcely noticed the difference when he really was not one. He spoke with equal warmth to common soldiers without regard to whether they addressed him as "Your Imperial Majesty" or "Citizen Romanov." He was distressed only when they would not speak to him at all. But he had no special faith in common men and he did not share the Tsaritsa's dream of future glory. He gave the impression, on the contrary, of being glad to be done once and for all with power and majesty. Nor did he adopt his wife's imperial attitude to the leaders of the revolution which had overthrown him. He disliked most of them but he treated them with a humble deference, and acted upon their orders almost invariably with an uncomplaining and respectful obedience. He had no faith in his new-found superiors. He had faith only in God and, as a recompense for all that he had lost, he only hoped that he himself would not be sent from Russia and that Russia would triumph over Germany in the war. Whether he recognized it or not, Nicholas appears to have shown no anxiety about the perilous position in which he and his family now found themselves. He had been calm in the presence of disaster before and now he was equally calm in the presence of his own disaster.

Such were the foundations of the heroic phase in the lives of Nicholas and Alexandra. Had it not been for their children, they would hardly have been disturbed by their impending tragedy.

The regime in the palace which had become a prison was a strange blend between court and captivity. Nicholas and Alexandra lived in their usual apartments and Count Benckendorff assiduously tried to insert himself between them and the facts of their new life. When the Tsar's presence was required by an official or a minister of the new government, the Count invariably represented to his master that the visitor was seeking an audience rather than the production of a prisoner. Kerensky himself has described how the screen was fabricated. He tells how, on his first visit to the Alexander Palace, he was conducted by Count Benckendorff into the imperial apartments. "The Count," he records, "was true to type. He left me standing face to face with a closed door and went in to announce me. Then he swung the double door wide open and said: 'His Majesty bids you welcome.' " [1]

This sort of thing, of course, was a pretense and a thin pretense at that. It was perhaps a way of conveying to Kerensky the profound contempt in which he was held by Benckendorff, but the Tsar naturally had no choice other than to bid him welcome and Kerensky naturally did pass through the double doors. He was in fact intoxicated with his sudden rise to fame and what he believed to be power. He was working off the inferiority complexes of a lifetime and in his own estimation he was a great and significant figure. Yet, on the brink of his first meeting with Nicholas II, he was, as he admits himself, uncertain of himself. "All the way along the endless chain of official apartments," he writes, "I was struggling for control over my emotions." [2]

Kerensky evidently had nurtured himself in the belief that the man he was about to meet was a monster of bloody oppression—a monster who had been caged by himself. Exalted and yet confused, he advanced through the double doors and received a shock:

> Through the door that Benckendorff had opened for me and through the open doorway into the next room, I immediately saw the Imperial family. They were standing slightly to the left of the entrance, nearer the window, around a small table, in a huddled, perplexed little group. From this cluster of frightened humanity there stepped out, somewhat hesitatingly, a man of medium height in military kit, who walked forward to meet me with a slight, peculiar smile. It was the Emperor. When he reached the door of the outer room, however, he stopped, in confusion. He did not know what to do, he did not know how *I* would act, what attitude I would adopt. Should he walk forward to meet me, as a host, or ought he to wait for me to speak first? Should he hold out his hand?
>
> In a flash, instinctively, I knew the exact position: the family's confusion, its fear at finding itself alone with a revolutionary whose objects in bursting in upon it were unknown, and finally, the awkward situation of Nicholas II. With an answering smile, I hurriedly walked over to the Emperor, shook hands and sharply said "Kerensky"—as I always do, by way of introduction, when meeting a man for the first time. Nicholas II gave my hand a firm grasp, immediately recovered from his confusion, and, smiling once again, led me to his family.[3]

What Kerensky had expected to receive from the Tsar he did receive from the Tsaritsa. "But Alexandra Feodorovna," he writes, "stood tense and erect—proud, domineering and irreconcilable; she held out her hand to me slowly and unwillingly. For my part, I found it equally hard to stretch out mine, and our fingers parted again after having scarcely touched." [4]

The firm handshake of the Tsar and the reluctant fingers of the Tsaritsa—the one a gesture of conciliation and of submission, the other a gesture of contempt and of defiance—were eloquent and revealing. Nicholas believed that the Provisional Government might save Russia and win the war. Alexandra believed that Russia was the monarchy and that Kerensky deserved to be hanged.

Kerensky himself was obviously well pleased by the figure he had cut. From the Tsar's hesitation he gained a sense of his power and from the Tsaritsa's reluctance a sense of his mission. But perhaps he deceived himself. The Tsar's own impression was a different one. He remarked later upon Kerensky's nervousness, at the beginning of the interview. He noticed how Kerensky raised his voice and flourished a paper cutter which he picked up while he was speaking. Only toward the end, he thought, did Kerensky calm down into cold civility. Nicholas too was well pleased with the interview and after it he placed much confidence in the man who was his jailer.

But, as he had so often been before, Nicholas was gravely mistaken in the object of his confidence. Kerensky was strutting across the stage of Russian history in peacock fashion. He was to leave no permanent mark and when he brandished a paper knife he was truly revealing the full extent of his real power. Even so his moment of glory was enough to seal the fate of the imperial family. Repeatedly he declared that no harm should come to the prisoners, but his power was not enough to honor the pledge and in the meantime his decisions, whether voluntary or otherwise, were to be the cause of grievous suffering for those to whom the hand of murder was being extended.

This first meeting between Kerensky and Nicholas II occurred on April 3rd. At almost the same time Lenin returned in triumph to Petrograd which, after a few more years, was to bear his name. The power of the Bolsheviks was growing and the collapse of the army, which they sought, was spreading. Already the Council of Workers' and Soldiers' Delegates had issued an order laying down that officers should not be saluted and that they should be elected by committees of their own men. Their agents were creeping along the battle fronts telling the peasant soldiers that there was about to be a great redistribution of the land and that they would do well to go home to receive the booty. Why, in any case, they asked, should the Russian workers fight against their brothers, the German workers? To an army which had suffered indescribable hardships and astronomical casualties, such advice had an electric effect. The Germans, indeed, had expected as much. Many of the Bolshevik leaders and agents were in their pay and it was they who had given Lenin back to Russia.

Gradually and ponderously the Russian peasant soldiers began to think about the principles of socialism and to listen to the declarations of Lenin. In their eyes the dawn of the new age seemed to offer them possession of the land, freedom from discipline, and the overthrow of all superior authority. To many of those at Tsarskoe Selo, and not always to the humblest among them, there seemed to be an opportunity for getting their own back. Colonel Kotsebue, the palace commandant, soon got into trouble. He was far too respectful to the imperial family and he was accused of having befriended Madame Vyrubova. He was removed and replaced by a less friendly successor, Colonel Korovichenko.

Colonel Kobylinsky, the garrison commander, tried to intervene to save the imperial family from unnecessary indignities, but his authority over his subordinates was always uncertain and constantly declining. Many of the more aggressive guards claimed that the Tsar was planning to escape and they repeatedly demanded to see the prisoners. Whenever they burst in upon him and his family, Nicholas invariably received these men in a friendly way but there were nevertheless several unpleasant scenes. On one such occasion, the Tsar, in his usual submissive way, held out his hand to a captain who had come to "inspect" him, but the officer turned away. Nicholas went up to him, put his hands on the man's shoulders and with tears in his eyes asked him, "Why did you do that?" The captain drew back and said, "I was born of common people and when they stretched out their hand to you, you did not take it, so now I will not shake hands with you." [5]

The pleasures of the guards were various. Some puffed tobacco smoke at the Tsaritsa's face. Others used obscene language in her presence and in that of the young Grand Duchesses. Another, seeing the Tsar on a bicycle in the grounds of the palace, inserted his bayonet into the spokes of one of the wheels and then expressed his amusement at the result. They also bullied the children. They confiscated a toy rifle to which Alexis was passionately devoted. They claimed that they could not allow the prisoners to be armed. When, however, Colonel Kobylinsky came upon the sobbing child he managed to smuggle his toy back to him.

Colonel Kobylinsky was not the only one who had some sympathy for the prisoners. Indeed, it was Colonel Korovichenko who secured for them the privilege of boating on the lake in the palace grounds, and though they were constantly followed by sentries while doing so, they were allowed to walk and to work in the gardens. Moreover, some of the guards, when they were brought face to face with their former ruler, found it impossible to reconcile what they had heard about him with what they could see in him. Some became more friendly and even respectful. But this was often the cause of further trouble. There was a fearful scene when the extremists heard that one of the ensigns had kissed the Tsaritsa's hand. Later, they elected a different kind of ensign, an Armenian named Domodziantz, as deputy to Colonel Kobylinsky. He gave orders to the guards prohibiting them from speaking to the prisoners, though he himself continued to do so and always in the most insulting terms.

Meanwhile the Provisional Government was conducting an elaborate inquiry into the conduct of the regime which it had overthrown. Among the objects of that inquiry there were naturally included the Tsar, the Tsaritsa, and members of their entourage. Kerensky himself supervised this part of the investigation, and that was the principal object of his many visits to Tsarskoe Selo. To the intense dismay of the Tsaritsa, he had Madame Vyrubova removed from the palace and incarcerated elsewhere, but, for lack of evidence about her political influence, she was later released. Kerensky also gave orders that while the inquiry lasted, the Tsar and the Tsaritsa were to be kept apart except at mealtimes when they were under supervision and were allowed to speak only in Russian which could be understood by their supervisors. He then initiated an investigation of their private papers. The object, apparently, was to incriminate them as pro-German.

At first, the investigators were hopeful. The Tsar picked up one of his letters saying that it was merely a private communication. At the same moment Colonel Korovichenko grabbed it and for an instant the accuser and the accused played tug of war with it. Then the Tsar recognized that he was not wanted and went for a walk. We are told by one of the Tsaritsa's ladies in waiting that in the last days of the monarchy the Tsaritsa burned a great many papers but that the Tsar burned none. This was not true. "Examined, Classified and burnt papers," the Tsar wrote in his diary on March 23rd.[6] He burned more the next day. Kerensky and his minions were unable to find anything suitable to their purpose and probably nothing of the kind ever existed. At any rate, after cross-examining the Tsaritsa, Kerensky condescended to tell the Tsar that his wife did not lie. Nicholas replied that he had always known that. Kerensky's investigation was not the last one which found that the Tsar's private papers were a poor weapon with which to belabor him. It seemed to many that after the investigation

Kerensky's attitude to the prisoners was more friendly than it had been before. All the same, he kept them as prisoners.

Whatever his motives may have been, his position was certainly a difficult one. Kerensky was trying to rule Russia without offending Lenin. Perhaps he was trying to save the imperial family without admitting it. The British ambassador, Sir George Buchanan, tells us that he was approached by the Provisional Government and asked to arrange an asylum in England for the Tsar, but that he was also asked not to publish the fact that this initiative had been taken by the Provisional Government. Sir George Buchanan says that he made such an arrangement and that on behalf of the British government, led at the time by Mr. Lloyd George, he extended a formal offer to the Provisional Government of an English asylum for the imperial family. It appears that a British warship was to come to a north Russian port to take on board the Tsar and his family and it even appears that the German government had undertaken not to interfere with that ship, which was to come through the Baltic. Kerensky claims that this offer was withdrawn before it could be exploited. Sir George Buchanan says that it was never withdrawn.

King George V undoubtedly was more than anxious to offer his country as an escape to his cousin. England after all was the traditional haven of the oppressed and the persecuted regardless of whether they were fallen monarchs like Louis XVIII, Louis Philippe, and Napoleon III, or hunted revolutionaries like Kossuth and Lenin himself. Mr. Lloyd George, however, was subjected to many pressures both political and emotional. Considerable sections of British public opinion were intensely hostile to the Tsar and even when he was down and out would not have welcomed his presence in England. The Prime Minister had to hold together a coalition government which, besides Liberals, included members of the Labour Party. There were also those who foresaw political difficulties in harboring the Tsar. Lord Bertie, the British ambassador in Paris, for example, pointed out that the Germans would be able to claim and the

Russian socialists might believe that the "British Government were keeping the ex-Emperor in reserve to be used for a restoration if it would suit the selfish policy of England to promote discord in Russia in the future." That, of course, might militate against the fighting alliance with Russia which, in spite of the monarchy's disappearance, was generally expected to continue. Moreover, Lord Bertie who, though an ambassador, evidently based his judgments upon tittle-tattle and newspaper gossip, added: "The Empress is not only a Boche by birth but in sentiment. She did all she could to bring about an understanding with Germany." [7]

Mr. Lloyd George nevertheless states in his memoirs that "the invitation was not withdrawn. The ultimate issue in the matter was decided by the action of the Russian Government, which continued to place obstacles in the way of the Czar's departure." [8] The initial obstacle, of course, was the illness of the imperial children, but after that Kerensky appears to have been reluctant to permit the Tsar's departure until he had completed the examination of his private papers. Then, after that examination had been completed, the danger of the Tsar being stopped or kidnaped by extremists while traveling to the port of embarkation was apparently mentioned as a further cause of delay.

There can be little doubt that the Provisional Government was hesitant and fearful of incurring the odium of arranging for the Tsar's departure to a secure exile. There can also be little doubt that the British government was anxious that its invitation should not be accepted. The irony of this disgusting tangle of political motives was that neither the Tsar nor the Tsaritsa wanted to go into a safe exile abroad. Months later, from Siberia, the Tsaritsa wrote to a friend: "Thank God, we are still in Russia and all together." [10] "I wouldn't leave Russia on any consideration," she was to tell M. Gilliard, "for it seems to me that to go abroad would be to break our last link with the past, which would then be dead for ever." [11] The Tsar had exactly the same attitude. One of the complications in any rescue attempt, M. Gilliard was to record in his diary after the imperial family had been transferred to Siberia, was that "he insists on two conditions which greatly complicate matters: he will not hear of the family being separated or leaving Russian territory." [12]

VIII

Siberia

NICHOLAS II had abdicated to save Russia and to keep the armies in the field. The belief that the armies could be kept in the field was widespread and it was one of the reasons for which the French and British governments welcomed the advent of the Russian revolution, and were reluctant even to protect the life of the fallen sovereign. It was also the reason for which the German government recognized that the revolution of March 1917 was inadequate and for which they harnessed their efforts toward the furtherance of a second revolution. Kerensky also believed that the armies could be kept in the field and he strained every nerve to inspire them with a fighting spirit. That was one of the reasons the Tsar not only tolerated but welcomed the dominating position which Kerensky appeared to have achieved in the new government.

The great Russian offensive which had been planned for the spring of 1917—the offensive which the Germans had so greatly feared and of which the allies had expected so much—did not take place. Russian attention at the time was concentrated not on Berlin but on Petrograd. Kerensky, however, was determined to repair the delay. In June he left for the front to practice his oratory upon the troops and on July 2nd the offensive began. At first it seemed to succeed and back at Tsarskoe Selo, the Tsar, who gleaned what news he could from the newspapers, showed his unqualified delight. But the Germans soon recovered from their surprise. Bolshevik propaganda had made its inroads upon the morale of the Russian army. The officers had lost their authority and the men had lost their will to win. The

German counterattack produced a Russian debacle not less complete and more permanent than that which had resulted from the battle of Tannenberg at the beginning of the war. Against Russia, the Germans now had a more powerful strategic weapon than their armies at the front. Lenin had chosen this moment to seize all power for the Soviets and to enact the international solidarity of the working classes.

Petrograd was seized by a second revolution which, for a moment, was on the verge of success. Kerensky returned from the front and acted with unusual vigor. Order was restored. Several Bolshevik leaders were arrested and Lenin, who sought not glory but power, disappeared into hiding in Finland. The revolution had failed and Kerensky became the head of the Provisional Government. The liberalism of Prince Lvov and his friends had also failed.

Kerensky, however, was now under fewer illusions than before. He was not the first to discover that it is easier to criticize an existing regime than to create a new one. "The Bolsheviks are after me," he told Nicholas, "and will be after you." [1] The ex-Tsar and the socialist prime minister were almost allies in the face of a common peril. "This man," Nicholas wrote of Kerensky in his diary, "is certainly in his right position at the present hour. The more power he gets, the better it will be." [2]

The motives and the actions of Kerensky are the sources of never-ending mystery. He had repressed the Bolshevik rising and arrested its leaders. Now he released them and returned to the path of appeasement. He had been at least reluctant to allow the Tsar to go into a safe exile abroad, but now he planned to transfer him to a safer imprisonment within Russia. Tsarskoe Selo had been far enough away from Petrograd, as Versailles had been from Paris, to allow the court to lose touch with the hub of affairs but, as Versailles also had been, it was not far enough away to escape the effects of an explosion at the hub. It seemed possible and even likely that Nicholas II, as a prisoner, would be confronted by the approach of the mob and borne away from the Alexander Palace as Louis XVI, while still king, had been borne away from the palace of Versailles nearly a hundred and thirty years earlier. Indeed, there was talk of a march on Tsarskoe Selo and there had already been an expedition of sorts which had, however, been satisfied by a sight of the ex-Tsar to prove that he had not escaped.

Kerensky evidently did not intend French history to be repeated in Russia. He decided to move the Tsar. Nicholas had always had a love for the Crimea and its agreeable climate and that is where he was hoping to be sent. But Kerensky had chosen differently. Siberia was the place to which the Tsars had traditionally expelled their opponents and it was to Siberia that Kerensky now determined to send the Tsar. Here again his action was mysterious, for the motive seems to have been a blend of the wish to protect the Tsar's life and the wish to avenge the suffering for which he and his ancestors had been responsible.

By this decision the repetition of French history in Russia was forestalled, but forestalled in a terrible way, for ultimately the surreptitious murder of Nicholas II in a Siberian cellar will surely rank as a worse crime that the public execution of Louis XVI at the heart of Paris in what is now, oddly enough, known as the Place de la Concorde.

Kerensky did not tell his prisoners where they were going. He merely told them that they were going. From his advice that they should supply themselves with plenty of warm clothing, it could, however, be inferred that they were not going to the Crimea. For some in the imperial entourage, the uncertain and apparently sinister prospect proved to be too much and for others there were better reasons for dropping out. The aged Count Benckendorff had to think of his sick wife; but though he now lost sight of his former sovereign, he never lost sight of the path of honor. Moreover, it was his own stepson, Prince Dolgoruky, who stepped into his place. The Baroness Buxhoeveden also had to drop out, for she was now in urgent need of an operation, but she too was still mindful of her duty and her allegiance. Later she was to return to her mistress and it was through no design of her own that she escaped the fate of those she served and loved.

The option which was given to the servants of the Tsar was also to some extent given to his children. Once more they had the chance of going south to their grandmother, who had not yet been molested. Once more they preferred to stay with their parents. That their decision was to cost them their lives could not be foreseen, but perhaps it was not entirely unsuspected. "What shall the future bring to my poor children?" the Tsaritsa wrote in a letter which she left for the Baroness Buxhoeveden. "My heart breaks thinking of them." [3]

On August 13, 1917, Kerensky came to Tsarskoe Selo to supervise the arrangements for the departure of the imperial family and their remaining entourage for an unknown destination. He had already decided that Colonel Kobylinsky should accompany them as commandant of the guards and the colonel had made his preparations. He had carefully selected the men who held the prisoners in the best esteem, but this, not unnaturally, had aroused the suspicions of those who were not selected and who held the prisoners in less esteem. When Kerensky arrived he was confronted with a difficult and even a dangerous situation. The extremists among the guards wanted to know where the Tsar was going and why they were not accompanying him. Kerensky declined to tell them but he had to argue with them for hours. So the night passed in confusion and uncertainty. All that time the young Tsarevitch, more asleep than awake, sat on a box holding his favorite pet, the spaniel called Joy. Meanwhile, and for the last time, the Tsar had dined with Count Benckendorff. They discussed the disposal of the firewood which had been cut by Nicholas, his family, and his servants during the summer months.

At last, in the early hours of August 14th, Kerensky prevailed. "The Emperor," Count Benckendorff recorded, "with great gravity, bade us a last good-bye, and this family of martyrs left the Palace, which had been their home for twenty-three years, for ever." [4] They walked out to the railway siding and with their retinue of about forty people, boarded the train which had been prepared for them. Shortly afterward it left. The imperial family was on the way to Tobolsk, one of the remotest towns to be found even in Russia.

Kerensky had told the military detachment that the prisoners were to be treated with courtesy and humanity. He had urged the soldiers not to strike at the captives when they were down. He had also taken steps to ensure that the journey should be a comfortable one. The cars in which the imperial family traveled were first class, but even if the journey could be made comfortable it could not be guaranteed to be safe. The Russian railways, as ever, were hazardous both for political and for mechanical reasons. Great care, however, was taken to conceal who was in the train and where it was going. The Japanese flag was displayed on its exterior.

While the train was in the vicinity of Petrograd there was always the danger that it might be stopped or attacked, but the farther east it traveled the less this danger became. When, three days after it had started, the end of the line was reached at Tiumen, the Tsar and his family found an atmosphere which was entirely different to the one they had left behind them. While they were transferred from the train to the river steamer *Rus* they were watched by a large crowd. There was silence but it was the silence of respect. People bowed and crossed themselves. Revolutionary ideas had not yet made much impression upon the region of the Ural Mountains.

The *Rus* then started down the river for Tobolsk, which was reached on August 19th. On the way it passed the village of Pokrovskoe in which could be seen the home of Rasputin—a fact which Nicholas forgot to record in his diary until later. It took over a month to prepare the governor's mansion for its new role as the imperial prison and during that time the prisoners remained in considerable comfort on board the *Rus*. Clearly, there was room for optimism. The local people appeared to be full of respect for their exalted and unexpected visitors. The revolution seemed to be a thousand miles away and Tobolsk, with its population of about twenty thousand people, was miles from anywhere. It had been bypassed by the trans-Siberian railway, which by making other places more accessible, had seemed to make Tobolsk less so. To Tobolsk, people and ideas came slowly and they came seldom. As far as the imperial family was concerned, Siberia fell far short of its sinister reputation.

Nor did August 26th, the day on which they were taken to the governor's mansion, do anything to belie the apparently improved prospect. The house was well and comfortably arranged. The people of Tobolsk raised their hats and often crossed themselves as well when they passed it. Most of the guards were well disposed and courteous to the captives. Colonel Kobylinsky even talked of allowing the Tsar out for shoot· ing expeditions. The only difficulty was that the house tended to be damp and, because there was no fuel for the elaborate central heating system, was likely to become intensely cold in a climate which often ran to fifty degrees of frost. There was, however, an especially agreeable surprise for the imperial family. With unexampled devotion, Mr. Gibbs, who had been unable to return to the Alexander Palace in Tsarskoe Selo, followed his master and his pupil into their Siberian exile and there he succeeded in rejoining them and his Swiss colleague, M. Gilliard.

Nicholas never was allowed to go shooting and the house did become intensely cold. Even the Tsaritsa, who had evidently inherited Queen Victoria's love of chilly and drafty rooms, felt it and suffered from chilblains as a result. Even so the family was able to settle down to a routine which, though restricted and monotonous, was far from harsh. They were permitted to cross the road in the mornings to attend church services and in the evenings services were held in the governor's mansion. The education of the three young Grand Duchesses and of the Tsarevitch was resumed. The Tsaritsa gave them religious instruction and also coached them in languages. The Tsar taught his son Russian history, though it may be doubted whether the events of his own reign were included in the syllabus. In addition the services of the two tutors were again available.

The Tsaritsa, who now constantly complained of heart trouble and other ailments, seldom came downstairs before lunch. She hardly ever went out and more often than not she dined upstairs with the Tsarevitch. The rest of the family was much more active. The Tsar, always a lover of physical exercise, applied himself vigorously to the cutting of firewood, in which he was often helped by the children and members of the suite. He established friendly relations with several of the guards and he and the Grand Duchesses often played draughts with them. In the evenings he usually read to the children and to those they were entertaining. This was a pastime which he had always enjoyed. Indeed, in many ways the quiet domesticity of the life was what Nicholas had always longed for and especially so since the outbreak of war when so often he had been separated from his family. To him the most distressing circumstance was the evident collapse of the Russian war effort, and it was this which began to make him think that he had been wrong to abdicate without a struggle. Now that he was so far from Petrograd and Moscow he may even have thought that he could have resisted the demand for his abdication. Nevertheless, and by comparison with the years of his reign as also by comparison with the imprisonment at Tsarskoe Selo, these first weeks in Tobolsk were, for Nicholas, practically idyllic. But the idyl was not to last.

In September, Kerensky dispatched two political commissars to Tobolsk. Both were members of the Social Revolutionary Party. The object of their mission no doubt was to allay extremist criticisms of the mildness with which the imperial prisoners were being treated, and if this was so, the two commissars were well chosen. The senior of them, a man named Pankratov, was hardly likely to be well disposed toward them. When he was eighteen, he had killed a policeman while defending a woman. For that he had been imprisoned for fifteen years and had subsequently been exiled to the Yakut district where he had lived for twenty-seven years. During the latter part of that time he had met and become friendly with Nikolsky, who had been exiled for disseminating revolutionary propaganda, and Nikolsky, the second of the two commissars sent to Tobolsk by Kerensky, was now Pankratov's assistant.

Pankratov, in spite of his violent action and its bitter consequences, was an easygoing man of mild disposition, weak character, and reasonably cultivated manners. The Tsar, indeed, always referred to him as "the little man." But his assistant. Nikolsky, was of a different kind. He was embittered, ill-mannered, obstinate, and vindictive. He was also a passionate revolutionary and it was he who abruptly ended the interlude of leniency in the captivity of the imperial family and initiated the persecution from which they were to be relieved only by death.

Nikolsky was horrified by the easy and friendly relations which existed between the Tsar and his jailers. That state of affairs did not at all correspond with his revolutionary principles. To remedy it, he lectured the soldiers upon the iniquities of the Tsarist regime and upon those of the Tsar and the Tsaritsa. He explained that there was no place in the brotherhood of man for former crowned heads or for their children. Some of the guards found it hard to be as rude to the prisoners as Nikolsky would have wished but others responded better. There was also a general collapse of military discipline and once again Colonel Kobylinsky found himself without any effective authority. Nikolsky saw to it that the regime in the governor's mansion was changed from one of house arrest to one of real prison. The privileges of the imperial family were progressively withdrawn and eventually they were not even allowed to go to church. Their activities were much more closely supervised and innumerable petty regulations and tribulations were thrust upon them. The Tsar was deprived of his dagger; a snow slide which the children had built in the garden was demolished; and once again obscene and insulting language was often on the lips of the soldiers. Their behavior worsened when the pay which Kerensky had promised them did not arrive.

This, however, was only a beginning. In November news arrived that Kerensky and the Provisional Government had been overthrown. This time the Bolshevik revolution had succeeded. But the Bolsheviks had their hands full and for the time being they left Tobolsk to look after itself. Nikolsky found that he had started something stronger than himself. The soldiers took the law into their own unco-ordinated hands and in February 1918 they dispensed with Pankratov and Nikolsky, both of whom they now regarded practically as reactionaries. They also dismissed their comrades of the Fourth Regiment who had continued to treat the imperial family with respect and courtesy. Nicholas and his family were thus left in the hands of a set of confused desperadoes whom Colonel Kobylinsky was powerless to control. Anything was liable to happen. The only order which came from Moscow was that the pay of the guards was to be increased from fifty kopeks to three rubles per day. That made Bolsheviks of them all.

The state of confusion which reigned in the governor's mansion at Tobolsk was, however, only a minor reflection of the far greater confusion which now beset the whole of Russia. The country had already fallen apart and was on the verge of a bitter and prolonged civil war. Some aspects of this complicated confusion were to have a decisive effect upon the fate of the imperial family and none more than the strange and remarkable activities of the Czechoslovak Legion.

In 1914, at the outbreak of war, a group of Czechs and Slovaks who were resident in Russia had organized a distinctive military detachment for service with the Russian army. Their passionate aim was the overthrow of the Hapsburg Empire and the re-establishment of their own country as a separate and sovereign state. During the war the Russians captured literally millions of Austrian troops and the easiest of all to capture were those of Czech or Slovak nationality who regarded the Russians as liberators and the Austrians as oppressors. In 1916 the Czech leaders, who had established their headquarters in Paris, proposed that the Czechoslovak detachment in the Russian army should be allowed to recruit these prisoners of war and bring them into action on the Russian side. The Tsar's government did not respond to the idea, but Kerensky's did, with the result that by December 1917 the Czechoslovak Legion in Russia consisted of some forty-five thousand resolute men.

By that time, however, the Russian army was disintegrating and the Bolshevik leaders who had recently come to power were already sounding out the Germans for an armistice. The Czechoslovak Legion withdrew to Kiev before the advancing Germans and submitted itself to the French supreme command. The intention was that it should be transferred from Russia to France and that it should continue the war against Austria and Germany from there. With that end in view, the Czechoslovak Legion sought the permission of the Soviet authorities to pass through their territory to Archangel and there to embark for France. They undertook to be neutral in the civil war which had already broken out in the Ukraine and elsewhere.

On February 16, 1918, the Bolshevik commander in the Ukraine accepted these conditions, but a few days later the Germans invaded the Ukraine and advanced rapidly. The Bolshevik commander, unable to stem the advance, appealed to the Czechoslovak Legion to resist it. The latter, however, was vastly outnumbered by the Germans and it began an immediate withdrawal eastward. The Germans blocked their retreat at Bakhmach but the Czechs extricated themselves after a three-day action in which they lost about six hundred men.

The future of the Czechoslovak Legion now became extremely confused. Trotsky, the Bolshevik commissar for war, was discussing with Britain and the United States the possibility of allied intervention on the side of the Red Army against the Germans. The Czechs, it was suggested, might be collected in the Murmansk area as a nucleus of this allied intervention.

The French, however, objected to this plan and it does not seem to have commended itself to Lenin, who was anxious to see the last of the Czechoslovak Legion. Then, on April 5, 1918, a Japanese force landed at Vladivostok. Lenin interpreted this as an allied intervention against the Red Army and immediately issued an order for all the Czech troop trains to be stopped. The Czechs resolved to meet any attempt to interfere with their movements by force and a state of war between the Red Army and the Czechoslovak Legion was imminent. By the end of April the Japanese were in occupation of Vladivostok, an anti-Bolshevik army of Cossacks was advancing along the railway to Harbin, the Czechoslovaks were strung out on the railway from Pensa to Omsk, and the Western allies were trying to decide whether they should intervene, and if so, on which side.

Eventually, after many conflicting orders, Trotsky gave instructions that the Czechoslovak Legion was to be disbanded and drafted into the Red Army. On May 25, 1918, he declared that the Czechs must lay down their arms and that any found with arms would be shot. The Czechs responded with force. They seized in rapid succession Penza, Syzran, and Samara, where they adhered to an anti-Bolshevik government which was proclaimed with their support. Farther to the east and considerably nearer to Tobolsk, they captured Cheliabinsk and, on June 7th, Omsk. As a result another anti-Bolshevik government, known as the Siberian Provisional Government, was proclaimed in Omsk.

No one was any longer master of all the Russias. The Bolsheviks under Lenin held power at the center but their writ did not run in huge areas of the perimeter, and notably in Siberia where he who had so recently been Tsar of all the Russias was confined. Prisoners who may be rescued, however, generally stand in greater peril than those who have no hope of escape. Neither the Czechs nor their associates, it is true, had any intention of attempting to restore the Russian monarchy, but they might well have released the ex-Tsar and his family from the horrors of a Bolshevik imprisonment. This the Bolsheviks themselves could not fail to recognize. The central government began to pay more attention to what was going on in Tobolsk. The prospect of being rescued by the Czechoslovak Legion reacted most unfavorably upon the fate of the unfortunate imperial family.

The movements of the Czechoslovak Legion and the outbreak of civil war in Siberia were not the only developments which, by offering the imperial family an apparent hope of escape, actually further endangered their already dangerous position. Ever since the arrest of the Tsar and the Tsaritsa there had been loyalist plans for their rescue. A kind of underground movement had been concerted and from time to time messages were slipped through to the prisoners, first at Tsarskoe Selo and then at Tobolsk, in which they were told that their rescue was imminent. But these messages, however well intentioned they may have been, were a cruel and horrible parody of the real situation. The underground movement, in which Madame Vyrubova and a number of singularly stupid ex-officers were concerned, was riddled with inertia and also, as it turned out, with treachery. The plans which it made were preposterous and there was never even a remote chance of their succeeding. The tragedy was that the imperial family, and especially the Tsaritsa, was led to believe that help was on the way, when in fact it was not even in prospect.

In the early days a plan was made for storming the Alexander Palace and releasing the prisoners. The guards were to be overcome with poisoned darts and the way to the Tsar was to be cleared with high explosives. It was perhaps as well that the project, like many others of its kind, never got beyond the talking stage. After the imperial family had been removed to Tobolsk, the underground loyalists adjusted their plans. They decided to send members of their organization into the area by ones and twos until a sufficient force had been accumulated. What the force was to be sufficient for was never clear. Nor were the activities and sometimes the motives of those sent much clearer. The first of their number appears to have been a man named Sedov, but after his departure nothing more was heard of him by the headquarters of the organization in Petrograd. After several months, they accordingly sent out another man whose name was Markov.

Markov had been a subaltern officer in the Tsaritsa's Own Crimean Cavalry Regiment. The Tsaritsa knew him personally. He was a brave man and there is no doubt that he was devoted to the persons of the two deposed sovereigns, but he was gullible by nature and roundabout by method. After an arduous and perilous journey, Markov reached Tobolsk in March 1918. He walked past the governor's mansion, saw the imperial family on the balcony and was apparently recognized by them. He sent them a message in which he told them that they would soon be rescued, but the basis of his assurance was nonexistent. He then withdrew to Tiumen in search of Sedov, whom he eventually found. He also found that Sedov had done nothing in the way of carrying out his mission. At Tiumen, Markov, like others who came out to help the imperial family, also met Solovev, who claimed to have the whole situation well in hand.

Solovev, one of the most mysterious of the many mysterious figures who crossed the Tsar's path, was Rasputin's son-in-law, having married the murdered *Staretz*'s daughter in October 1917. Undoubtedly he was in touch with the Tsaritsa, who was naturally inclined to accept his credentials as impeccable, but he was also in receipt of not inconsiderable sums of money contributed by loyalists for the benefit of the imperial family. He was also thought to be in the pay of the Germans and perhaps of the Bolsheviks as well. However that may have been, he does appear to have denounced to the Bolshevik authorities loyalists who would not submit to his direction. At any rate, Markov seems to have taken Solovev at his own word.

The upshot was that nothing of any kind was done for the imperial family. Markov eventually concluded that only the

Germans could save them, and it was to the Grand Duke of Hesse, the Tsaritsa's brother, that he finally made his appeal—after the Tsaritsa had been murdered. There were few who had the wish and none who had the ingenuity to save the imprisoned and persecuted imperial family. Truly, the imperial family had been deserted and left to the mercy of those who hated it. Almost its only friends were in prison with the family.

Nevertheless, and however feeble they may have been, the activities of the underground loyalists gave the Bolshevik authorities further grounds for increasing the stringency of the imperial imprisonment, and eventually for worse than that.

The Germans, indeed, might have saved the imperial family. They now represented the greatest single and by far the most highly organized power in Russia. The Bolshevik policy of peace at almost any price and the collapse of the former Imperial Russian Army had saved the Germans from what would have been a devastating and possibly even a decisive offensive in 1917. It had enabled them to overrun vast areas of Russia and to gain access to untold agricultural and mineral resources. It had enabled them to consolidate their position by the conclusion of the famous Peace of Brest-Litovsk, signed on March 3, 1918, by which the Russians lost the conquests of three centuries. Their ambassador in Moscow, Count Mirbach, had to be listened to with respect. From Russia under its new rulers, the Germans had nothing to fear except the idea of bolshevism which they themselves, for strategic reasons, had done so much to establish in power. There was no reason save that of honor between sovereigns and between cousins—who had never liked each other—for which the Germans should endanger their position in Russia by supporting the loyalists in their attempts to rescue the imperial family. Indeed, when he appealed to Count Mirbach, Count Benckendorff received an exceedingly cool response. The Germans could hardly afford to take risks for sentimental reasons when they were confronted in the West by a military alliance invigorated by the accession of the United States of America.

Moreover, the Germans quite obviously could not look with favor upon the activities of the Czechoslovak Legion. Not only was it dedicated to the destruction of their own ally, the Hapsburg monarchy, but it was the nucleus of a new Russian front which the Western allies hoped to form against the Germans. For all but ideological reasons, the Bolshevik regime in Russia was the one which suited the Germans, and in 1918 they were not in a position to be overscrupulous about ideological factors.

Nor, even on ideological grounds, could they hope to gain anything by rescuing the Tsar. It was clear that he could never be effectively restored to the Russian throne. Even so, it does seem that the Germans did play some part in the final phase of the imperial tragedy. What that part was cannot at present be established.

Here then were three influences—the activities of the Czechoslovak Legion, the escape "plans" of the loyalists, and the pressure of the Germans—which were presently to have an effect upon the life of the imperial prisoners of Tobolsk. In addition to them and partly because of them, there was another factor to be considered. This factor was the local development of bolshevism in Siberia which, because of the general chaos, was not always quite in gear or even in touch with the central government at Moscow.

When he arrived at Tobolsk in August 1917 the Tsar had been received by the local people very much as he would have been if he had still been on the throne. Revolutionary ideas tended to travel along the railways and there was no railway to Tobolsk. Nor in the vast spaces of Siberia were there many roads worth the name. To the inhabitants of the innumerable and primitive little villages, which consisted of no more than groups of tiny huts, Moscow and Petrograd were part of the outside world as unknown and as unheard of as London, Paris, New York, or Tokyo. Most of the people had not even the means of judging the difference between an Englishman and a Japanese. But there were certain exceptions to this general state of affairs—exceptions created by the trans-Siberian railway which had been driven right through the heart of this gigantic wasteland.

The most important exception to the Siberian rule was provided by the town of Ekaterinburg which lay some two hundred and eighty miles to the west-southwest of Tobolsk and nearly a thousand to the east of Moscow. Ekaterinburg was a special case because it was a focal point on the trans-Siberian railway, the point at which the line from Vladivostok divided for Moscow and Petrograd; and because it was the center of important industrial activities. Ekaterinburg, in fact, had both communications and a factory proletariat. It was among the first of the provincial towns to welcome the Petrograd revolution of March 1917 by which the Tsar was deposed, and again it was among the first and the most enthusiastic supporters of the Bolshevik revolution in November.

But Ekaterinburg did not merely follow the trend of affairs at the center. It also rapidly developed its own Bolshevik fervor and Bolshevik institutions. Among the first of the aims of the Ekaterinburg Soviet was the determination that the Tsar should not escape. In this matter, the Ekaterinburg Soviet was not content to leave all the decisions in the hands of the central government; it was jealous of the activities of other local Soviets, as for example that at Omsk, and it was certainly not prepared to leave the garrison at Tobolsk to its own devices.

Nor were the soldiers at Tobolsk prepared to be left to their own devices any more than they were willing to obey the orders of their now-nominal commandant, Colonel Kobylinsky. Undisciplined but suspicious, they were chiefly concerned about their pay which, in spite of the promises made by the Bolshevik government, still was not arriving. Commissars from Ekaterinburg and from Omsk had already come to Tobolsk and, in competition with each other, were trying to paint the backward town slightly different shades of red, but the soldiers who guarded the governor's mansion were now demanding the dispatch of a commissar from Moscow, and in the middle of March they sent one of their number, Peter Loupin, to Moscow to see that their demand was met. Loupin returned on April 12th and announced that a commissar would shortly be arriving. There was even a rumor that Trotsky himself was on the way.

Meanwhile, the conditions in which the prisoners were living became steadily worse. In February, the central government had given orders for the comforts and privileges of the imperial family to be drastically reduced. They were put onto soldiers' rations and their budget was curtailed to such an extent that many of the servants had to be discharged. The guards, of their own volition, insisted upon the removal of the imperial epaulets from the Tsar's uniform and Colonel Kobylinsky could think of nothing better to say to them than that they should treat their prisoner with more respect because he was a cousin of the King of England.

There was indeed little or nothing which Colonel Kobylinsky could do to moderate the behavior of the guards and if the Tsar had not begged him to stay on as his last friend, he would probably have resigned and gone, as he later did go, to fight the Bolsheviks in the field. Meanwhile, the arrival of the commissar from Moscow was awaited with curiosity and, by the imperial family, with apprehension. Nicholas was deeply distressed by the collapse of the Russian army and he was disgusted by the treaty of Brest-Litovsk, which he regarded as a dishonor without parallel in Russian history—a dishonor incurred by the very people who had once accused his wife of being a pro-German traitor. Moreover, it was clear to the imperial family that their days of relative immunity from the revolution were over. "Though we know that the storm is coming nearer," the Tsaritsa wrote to Madame Vyrubova at the beginning of April, "our souls are at peace. Whatever happens will be through

God's will. Thank God, at least, the little one is better." [5] At last, and none too soon, the Tsaritsa had acquired something of her husband's lifelong fatalistic resignation.

The Siberian climate was not a good one in which to recover from whooping cough but that is what the Tsarevitch, "the little one," was now struggling to do. No sooner had he done so than he succumbed to a severe attack of hemophilia, the worst he had had since 1912 when at Spala. He was never to make a complete recovery.

Such was the situation when, on the evening of April 22, 1918, the commissar from Moscow arrived. His name was Vassili Vassilievitch Yakovlev.

Yakovlev, who was dressed in the uniform of a naval rating and appeared to be in his early thirties, was accompanied by a mounted bodyguard of a hundred and fifty men. He put up for the night in Kornilov's house on the opposite side of the road to the governor's mansion and the next morning, when he called on Colonel Kobylinsky, it appeared that he was a man of considerable importance. He produced papers signed by Sverdlov, an old associate of Lenin's and now, as Chairman of the Central Executive Committee in Moscow, one of the most powerful men in the Bolshevik hierarchy. Yakovlev's papers showed that he was empowered to take absolute charge of the imperial prisoners and they enjoined both Colonel Kobylinsky and the Tobolsk garrison to carry out his orders on pain of death.

Yakovlev spent much of the day of April 23rd in impressing this last point upon the soldiers who, from the first, were somewhat suspicious of his intentions. He also saw the Tsar, who for different reasons was no less suspicious, and he showed a great interest in the Tsarevitch's health. Several times he went to Alexis' bedside and stared intently at the child, who was half paralyzed and suffering agonies. Evidently Yakovlev foresaw and was anxious to forestall opposition from the Tobolsk soldiers and, equally evidently, the Tsarevitch's illness was an obstacle to his plans. But what his plans were, and indeed who Yakovlev really was, were unknown and may never be known. By the imperial family and by those who still stood beside them, Yakovlev's arrival was felt "to be an evil portent, vague but real." [6]

IX

Separation and Reunion

WHOEVER Yakovlev may have been, he obviously was no ordinary sailor. He spoke French fluently and it seemed that he also knew English and German. The way in which he addressed the mutinous soldiers of the Tobolsk garrison suggested to those who looked on that he was used to the exercise of authority and, more strangely still, he treated the Tsar with the utmost respect, bowing and saluting more in the manner of an imperial officer than a Bolshevik commissar. It was all very strange and, to Colonel Kobylinsky, very encouraging. Colonel Kobylinsky, in fact, came to the conclusion that Yakovlev was not an agent of bolshevism at all but that he had come to rescue the imperial family. He was, therefore, neither surprised nor dismayed when, on the morning of April 25th, Yakovlev told him that he had indeed come to remove the imperial family from Tobolsk.

At two o'clock that afternoon, Yakovlev and Colonel Kobylinsky entered the hall of the governor's mansion. The Tsar and the Tsaritsa stood in the middle of the floor. Yakovlev bowed to them and then, addressing himself to the Tsar only, explained that he had been sent by the Moscow Central Executive Committee to remove the imperial family from Tobolsk. He said that since his arrival, he had been in touch with Moscow by telegram and in view of the Tsarevitch's illness, had been ordered to remove only the Tsar himself. He said nothing of where he intended to take the Tsar but Nicholas interrupted and said that he refused to go. Yakovlev begged him not to make difficulties, saying that, in such an event, he would either have to use force or resign. If he resigned, he added, the Central

Executive Committee would probably send some less scrupulous commissar to carry out their orders. Yakovlev assured the Tsar that he had nothing to fear and he vouched with his own life for that of his prisoner. He told the Tsar that if he did not want to go alone he could take anyone he liked with him, but he must be prepared to go, accompanied or alone, by four o'clock the next morning. Yakovlev then bowed again to the imperial couple and they left the hall without the Tsar saying anything more.

Colonel Kobylinsky was almost jubilant. More than ever he was convinced that Yakovlev was only posing as a Bolshevik commissar. He, like the Tsar himself, had not been told the destination of the journey, but Yakovlev had mentioned to him that it would take three or four days, and on that basis, the Colonel had assumed that the destination was Moscow. There was a rumor, apparently put about by Yakovlev himself, that Lenin had ordered the Tsar to Moscow with the object of putting him on trial but, for reasons which he did not explain, Colonel Kobylinsky did not believe that there would be a trial. He had apparently convinced himself that the journey would continue directly toward Finland and that it would end in England.

Possibly Colonel Kobylinsky had an exaggerated idea of the influence of King George V in Russia, or he had a false impression of the attitude of Lenin, or it may be that he had over-persuaded himself in an attempt to assuage his own conscience in handing over Nicholas, with whom he genuinely sympathized, to the unknown and mysterious Yakovlev. Nevertheless, it was as a result of his interpretation that Dr. Botkin, the Tsaritsa's physician, decided to pack his tennis flannels which he thought would be indispensable for a stay in England.

Nicholas himself, however, did not share Colonel Kobylinsky's optimism, nor, even if he had shared the colonel's interpretation, would he have regarded it as a basis of optimism. Even at this desperate hour, he had no wish to go into a foreign exile. He wanted to stay in Russia—even the Russia of the

revolution. Nor was Nicholas much impressed by the assurance
Yakovlev had given him about the security of his own life. It
was not that he had any special reason to distrust it. It was
simply that he had no particular concern about his life, which
was in the hands of God—not of Yakovlev. Nicholas did agree
with Colonel Kobylinsky that the probable destination of the
journey was Moscow, and he also agreed that Yakovlev was
probably not really a Bolshevik commissar. He believed, in
fact, that Yakovlev was a German agent and that the object of
taking him to Moscow was to force him to sign the treaty of
Brest-Litovsk.

The Tsaritsa too thought that this was a likely explanation.
"They're going to try to force his hand by making him anxious
about his family," she told M. Gilliard. "The Czar is necessary
to them," she said, "they feel that he alone represents Russia." [1]

However unlikely or unrealistic this view may have been,
it was the natural one for the Tsaritsa to take. How, indeed,
could anyone other than the Tsar represent Russia and, since
no one had acceded to the throne after Nicholas' abdication,
how could anyone other than Nicholas II be regarded as the
Tsar of Russia? The Germans, no doubt, took a different view,
though it is not impossible that they wished to have Nicholas
somewhere other than Siberia where the symptoms of a new
allied front against themselves were growing more pronounced.
But however that may have been, the important thing to the
Tsaritsa, of course, was her own interpretation and her own
expectation. They placed her in an agonizing position and
confronted her with the most searing decision she had ever had
to make.

Nicholas declared that he would sooner cut off his right hand
than sign the infamous treaty of Brest-Litovsk but the Tsaritsa,
convinced no doubt of the sincerity of his purpose, was less
sure of his strength to carry it out. So many times before, when
she had not been there to support him, he had given in. After
all, he who had signed the Constitution of October 1905 and
the Act of Abdication in March 1917, might in the end sign

the treaty of Brest-Litovsk in May 1918. She felt it her absolute duty to go with him on the journey for which Yakovlev was now making feverish preparations. But if she went she would have to leave her son who was desperately ill. Indeed, while she was with the Tsar in the hall listening to Yakovlev's orders and explanations, Alexis was calling to her from upstairs.

But she could not bear to go up. "For the first time in my life," she told M. Gilliard, "I don't know what I ought to do; I've always felt inspired whenever I've had to take a decision, and now I can't think." [2] All she could hope was that a sudden thaw would set in and make the river impassable so that the journey could not begin. "But God won't allow the Czar's departure; it can't, it *must* not be. I'm sure the thaw will begin tonight," [3] she said, though perhaps more in desperation than in hope.

It was intensely cold and there was no sign of a thaw. It was clear that God was going to allow the Tsar's departure and suddenly the Tsaritsa made her decision. "I must leave my child and share the life or the death of my husband." [4] She went straight up to Alexis' room.

Afterwards it was arranged that the Tsar and Tsaritsa should be accompanied by their third and strongest daughter, the Grand Duchess Marie, the Tsaritsa's physician, Dr. Botkin, her maid, Anna Demidova, the marshal of the court, Prince Dolgoruky, the Tsar's valet, Chemodurov, and the young waiter, Sednev. Yakovlev showed little interest in who was going. His interest was in the Tsar and in a rapid departure. Already he had sent one of his assistants ahead to arrange about a train from Tiumen, which was as near as the railway got to Tobolsk.

The name of this assistant was Avdeiev. He wore a sort of military uniform, appeared to be in his late twenties or early thirties, had a thin pale face, and was dirty and uncouth. Presumably Yakovlev knew that Avdeiev was a man of some importance and influence in Ekaterinburg. He was, in fact, the head of a factory there which, in December 1917, he had commandeered from its owner, Nicholas Zlokazov who, as a result of Avdeiev's action, was now in prison.

Meanwhile the imperial family awaited the execution of Yakovlev's plan. "The Czarina," M. Gilliard recorded, "was seated on the divan with two of her daughters beside her. Their faces were swollen with crying. We all did our best to hide our grief and to maintain outward calm. We felt that for one to give way would cause all to break down. The Czar and Czarina were calm and collected.... They have never shown greater kindness or solicitude. This splendid serenity of theirs, this wonderful faith, proved infectious." [5]

At half past eleven that night all the servants were assembled in the hall where the Tsar, the Tsaritsa, and the Grand Duchess Marie came to thank them and bid them good-by. The Tsar embraced every man and the Tsaritsa every woman. These were the faithful people who had remained loyal after the ruin of their master and mistress and had accompanied them into their Siberian imprisonment. Almost all were in tears. There were not many of their kind in Russia. But the Tsar and the Tsaritsa were not only grateful to their faithful servants. They were also grateful to their jailer, Colonel Kobylinsky. The Tsaritsa blessed him and the Tsar spoke a few words of friendly gratitude.

The night wore on into the early morning and at four o'clock the Tsar and Tsaritsa went upstairs to say good-by to and to embrace their little son, who was so ill but not so ill as to be unaware that he was being left. The Tsaritsa begged M. Gilliard to stay with the boy and he went straight to his room, where he found him sobbing. A few minutes later he heard the clatter of wheels and the three Grand Duchesses came upstairs and passed their brother's room. They too were sobbing.

The journey had begun in Siberian springless carts. Each one, as its only comfort, had a little straw at the bottom of it, but already Yakovlev had suffered a setback. The Tobolsk soldiers had become more and more suspicious of his intentions, and had insisted upon joining the convoy. Yakovlev, evidently more anxious to start than to argue, had agreed that eight of them should do so. In this way the Tsar and the Tsaritsa left Tobolsk for they knew not where. It was their strangest journey and it was also their last. They simply clattered off into the dark and the cold surrounded by horsemen.

Yakovlev drove forward at the greatest possible speed but the going was frightfully difficult and the carts were by no means robust. Sometimes the wheels flew off and at others the harness broke but Yakovlev headed for Tiumen like a man determined to get there and he did, on the evening of April 27th, some forty hours after leaving Tobolsk. On the way the convoy had stopped only briefly to seek shelter and rest in peasant huts.

Meanwhile, those who had remained behind in the governor's mansion at Tobolsk were anxiously awaiting news. Even under ordinary circumstances a journey of this kind was a hazardous undertaking and at this time of year it was also a grueling one. On the morning of April 28th Colonel Kobylinsky received a telegram which showed that the expedition had reached Tiumen. Later on the same day he received another, signed by Yakovlev, but obviously sent on behalf of the Tsar and Tsaritsa, asking after the "Little One" and saying that the journey was going well. Further and similar messages were received on the morning of April 29th but then nothing more was heard for four days, and the message which then arrived had a stupefying effect. It came from one of the soldiers of the Tobolsk detachment and without giving any explanation or any details it simply said that the train had been stopped at Ekaterinburg where the Tsar, the Tsaritsa, their daughter, and the other prisoners had been seized.

What had happened was this. When the expedition reached Tiumen a luxurious train, including a first-class sleeping car of the Samara-Zlatoonst line, was found to be in readiness. Yakovlev boarded it with his prisoners and it started immediately in a westerly direction along the line toward Ekaterinburg. But before it got there, Yakovlev seems to have anticipated trouble ahead. He had the train reversed and it set off for Omsk. At Omsk there was a junction from which another line led westward through Cheliabinsk and it may have been Yakovlev's intention to follow this with the object of bypassing Ekaterinburg. But whether this was so or not, he never had the opportunity, for at Koulomzino, the last station before Omsk, the train was stopped and surrounded by Red soldiers. Yakovlev was told that it would not be allowed to go on to Omsk. Yakovlev himself went on there and apparently made contact with the central government in Moscow by whom, it seems, he was told to take the prisoners to Ekaterinburg. Once more the train was reversed and once more it started westward toward Ekaterinburg. When it got there it was again surrounded by Red soldiers. The Tsar, the Tsaritsa, their daughter, and their fellow prisoners were taken off it and driven away in the direction of the town. Yakovlev sent a telegram to those of his men whom he had left in Tobolsk in which he said that he had resigned and could not be held responsible for whatever the consequences might be. It seems that he then returned to Moscow and so far as is known was not heard of again, though some say that he later fought in the White Army against the Bolsheviks. Avdeiev, the assistant whom Yakovlev had sent ahead to Tiumen, was soon saying in Ekaterinburg that Yakovlev had intended to take the Tsar out of Russia and that the attempt had been foiled only by his own action in warning the Ekaterinburg Soviet in good time.

This may well have been true. Whether it was or not, preparations for the imprisonment of the Tsar in Ekaterinburg had been made well in advance of his arrival there. A house belonging to an engineer named Ipatiev had been commandeered and around it a large wooden stockade had been erected. It was to this house that the imperial prisoners were taken and the commandant of the guards there was none other than Avdeiev himself.

So now the Tsar, the Tsaritsa, and their daughter were in the hands of a man whom Colonel Kobylinsky had described as dirty and uncouth, and who, as one of his subordinates observed, never lost an opportunity of drinking a kind of alcoholic yeast paste which he got at the Zlokazov factory of which he was the head. Avdeiev knew all the correct Bolshevik phrases about the imperial family. He called the Tsar a "blood drinker" and told the men he recruited from his factory to act as guards at Ipatiev's house that Nicholas had delighted in the slaughter of the war and thrived upon shooting down Russian workers. Moreover, it paid the men in the Zlokazov factory to agree with Avdeiev's views. He could provide easygoing jobs in the works and those who volunteered for the guard at Ipatiev's house received extra pay. The outlook for the prisoners in Ekaterinburg was bleak.

Nor was the position of those who had remained in Tobolsk much better. Colonel Kobylinsky was no longer allowed into the governor's mansion and the control there was assumed, nominally at least, by one of the men who had come with Yakovlev. His name was Rodionov and he had a mysterious past. One of the friends of the imperial family, General Tatishchev, who had come with them to Tobolsk, thought he had seen him before. Years before, the general had been temporarily attached to the entourage of the Kaiser in Berlin and it was in Berlin that he thought he had seen Rodionov's face. But when he asked him what his former profession had been, Rodionov said that he could not remember. Whatever the explanation of this may have been, the new commandant now showed little sympathy with the prisoners. His orders evidently were to have them transferred to Ekaterinburg as soon as possible, and he repeatedly pressed Dr. Derevenko, who was treating the Tsarevitch, to declare that his patient was fit to travel. The doctor protested but when, on May 16th, Rodionov saw Alexis sitting in a chair, he gave orders for the journey to start the next day. The sick boy had hardly been out of bed since April 12th, but it was only with great difficulty that Dr. Derevenko got a postponement of the journey, and then he only got a postponement of four days.

Rodionov was fond of declaring that he had been born in prison by the grace of the Tsar. He was also fond of making conditions for the three Grand Duchesses and the Tsarevitch as harsh and as humiliating as possible. He even forbade the girls to lock their door at night. In his errand of the opposite of mercy, he was accompanied by Khokhriakov, possibly the more brutal of the two. It was not clear which was the senior and which was the assistant, but the result of their regime was horrifying and especially so in the course of the journey to Ekaterinburg which began on May 20th.

It was still bitterly cold but the river was again navigable and, for the journey to Tiumen, the steamer *Rus* on which, almost a year earlier, the family had come to Tobolsk was put into service. But the *Rus* in charge of Rodionov was hardly the same ship as it had been in charge of Colonel Kobylinsky. Colonel Kobylinsky himself was now disillusioned, powerless, and ill in bed.

The journey started with an announcement to the prisoners by Rodionov that life in future was going to be much harder for them. This was one of the few assurances to them which was honored in full. Alexis still could not walk and he had to be carried on board by his faithful and heroic attendant, the sailor Nagorny, but after that he was allowed no more attention. The three girls were bundled into cabins and allowed no privacy. Also on board were several of their few remaining friends—General Tatishchev, Dr. Derevenko, Countess Hendrikova, Baroness Buxhoeveden, Mlle. Schneider, the former "Court Reader," M. Gilliard, Mr. Gibbs, and a number of servants. All, of course, were prisoners.

At Tiumen there was an argument with the local Bolshevik authorities but eventually Rodionov put all his prisoners into a dingy train which consisted partly of passenger coaches and partly of freight cars, and the last stage of the last journey was begun. The train reached Ekaterinburg early in the morning. It was very cold and wet. For hours the train shunted to and fro but at last it stopped between two stations. The scene there was described by M. Gilliard.

"Several carriages were drawn up alongside our train," he wrote, "and I saw four men go towards the children's carriage. A few minutes passed and then Nagorny, the sailor attached to Alexis Nicolaïevitch, passed my window, carrying the sick boy in his arms; behind him came the Grand-Duchesses, loaded with valises and small personal belongings. I tried to get out, but was roughly pushed back into the carriage by a sentry. I came back to the window. Tatiana Nicolaïevna came last, carrying her little dog and struggling to drag a heavy brown valise. It was raining, and I saw her feet sink into the mud at every step. Nagorny tried to come to her assistance; he was roughly pushed back by one of the commissaries. . . . A few minutes later the carriages drove off with the children in the direction of the town." [6]

Neither M. Gilliard nor Mr. Gibbs were allowed to follow. They, and more strangely the Baroness Buxhoeveden as well, were taken off the train and turned out of the district. Though they thus escaped the terrible fate of the family they had served and that of many of their colleagues, they have surely earned an honorable place in the ageless annals of courage and of devotion.

This scene beside the train at Ekaterinburg was nearly the end of many other things. Nagorny had rendered almost his last service to the Tsarevitch and he had made almost his last gesture to the Grand Duchesses. Like the imperial children whom he had tried to help, he had less than two months in which to live, for in the final act the Bolsheviks, as they did not distinguish between father and children, also did not distinguish between master and servant.

For the final act, however, the Tsar and the Tsaritsa were reunited with all of their five children.

X

The House of Special Purpose

THAT the last prison of Nicholas II, the last of the Romanov Tsars, should have been called Ipatiev's house was an extraordinary coincidence, for it was from Ipatiev's Monastery that Michael Feodorovitch, the first of the Romanov Tsars, had been called to the throne three centuries earlier. But there was something more sinister than this coincidence about the new imperial prison and that was the title by which it was now known—the House of Special Purpose.

What that special purpose would be was easily suspected by the prisoners. They knew that they had reached the hour of "utmost dread"; that they were "on the threshold of the grave." [1] But in their final agony they were denied even the comforts of a common murderer in the condemned cell who knows he will die on the morrow. In Ipatiev's house the imperial prisoners were subjected not only to a deliberate and a vile persecution but they were flung from the prospect of death to the hope of rescue and back again with merciless cruelty. In addition, the little Tsarevitch had to bear agonies of pain from his illness, which at this time may well have been killing him, and on his behalf his family had to suffer equal agonies of anxiety. Yet on all the evidence which can be found, the whole family passed through this frightful and ultimate ordeal calmly, with dignity, almost with indifference and, above all, in the spirit of forgiveness. Avdeiev was the commandant who normally answered any remark addressed to him about the Tsar with the phrase "Let him go to hell," he was the man who reeled about stupefied by drink in the presence of the Tsaritsa, the man who posted sentries to watch the Grand Duchesses in the lavatory, and the man who helped himself liberally to the personal possessions of the prisoners. Yet when he was dismissed by his superiors all that Nicholas could think of to record in his diary was that it was "a pity" for Avdeiev.[2]

"My poor Tsar," one of Nicholas's former officers, who at this moment was trying to rescue him, later wrote, "if only he had been a little less kind, a little more brutal, a little less thoughtful for those around him, a little more ruthless for the sake of those he never saw, if only he had known how to fight and rule as well as he knew how to pray."[3] Whether or not another kind of Tsar could have found himself in a better place than Nicholas was in, he could not have found himself in a worse. However that may have been, in that place it was certainly more important to know how to pray than how to fight. At last, the fatalistic resignation of the Tsar and the hysterical mysticism of the Tsaritsa, the very qualities which had denied them success on the throne, came to their rescue and, through them, to the rescue of their children. The guards in Ipatiev's house, between the verses of the obscene and revolutionary songs which they sang downstairs, could often, as some of them afterward remembered, hear other voices upstairs. These were the voices of the imperial family raised up in the rendering of hymns. All was in the hands of God and, united by love and united in faith, the imperial family was undaunted and unassailable. This was the hour of their glory, and it was a glory which would have been denied them if they had been shipped off to decay in some foreign exile. There was, after all, no homeland to which any of them could have gone. The Tsar's mother came from Denmark and there eventually she was able to return to end her days, but neither the Tsar nor his children had any home outside Russia and the Tsaritsa had declared that she would rather die in Russia than be saved by the Germans.

The Tsarevitch arrived at Ipatiev's house in very poor condition. He had by no means recovered from the severe attack of hemophilia which he had suffered in Tobolsk and almost immediately after the journey, he jarred his leg and was further incapacitated by an internal hemorrhage. His attendant, Nagorny, was removed to the town prison in Ekaterinburg, where he was presently murdered, and his doctor, Derevenko, was excluded from the household and only allowed to visit his patient under the supervision of the guards. The Tsarevitch never walked again but was always carried by his father or one of his so much more robust sisters. One of them, the Grand Duchess Marie, immediately gave up her bed to him, for there were not at first enough beds to go round. In the meantime the girls slept on the floor.

The prisoners were allowed to exercise in the small garden but apart from that they had practically no liberty of action and not much more privacy. In addition to the sentries posted around the outside of the house, several were posted inside it, including one who stood at the lavatory door. The commandant, Avdeiev, occupied a room on the first floor, the same floor on which were the rooms allotted to the prisoners. A few of his men shared it with him and others were quartered downstairs. The prisoners' food was brought from a local communal kitchen and was deficient both in quality and in quantity. Moreover, it was a common occurrence for a sentry to remove the best of it from under the noses of the imperial family. The prisoners were not allowed to go to church, but from time to time a priest was admitted to the house to hold a service there. Several cases containing possessions of the family were stored downstairs and Avdeiev and some of his friends soon began to help themselves to the contents.

Meanwhile, the imperial family with Dr. Botkin, the maid, Anna Demidova, and a few other faithful servants awaited the turn of fate. They were practically in the front line of a war between the Whites and the Reds, and the Whites were advancing. They heard by various means of loyalist plans to rescue them and they must have recognized that there seemed to be a chance of escape. On one particular night they evidently

believed that the chance was imminent. At any rate they remained dressed and alert all night, but nothing happened. By
the beginning of July they could hear the sound of artillery
fire which heralded the approach of the Czechoslovak Legion.
But the Bolsheviks, of course, could hear the same sounds and
the louder they became the more stringent the conditions in
the House of Special Purpose became.

Avdeiev had recruited most of the guards for the House of
Special Purpose from two of the local factories, his own, the
Zlokazov, and the Sissert Works. Most of these men had nothing
to make them regret the passing of the old regime and much to
hope for from the advent of the new one. The senior man
among those brought from Zlokazov factory was Anatoly Yakimov and the senior man from Sissert's was Paul Medvedev.
Yakimov was thirty years old and was a native of the Perm
district where his father had a job at the Motoviliha Works.
By comparison with most of his companions, Yakimov had had
an excellent education. For three years, from the age of eight,
he had been at a school attached to an ecclesiastical seminary.
He went on to a more advanced school but, when he was twelve,
his father died. Because of a lack of money and, as he put it
himself, because of a lack of interest in education, he left school
soon afterward and took a job as a bellboy in the drafting room
of the Motoviliha Works. When he was sixteen, he transferred
to the machine shop and began to learn the skilled processes of
milling. In 1906 he married the daughter of a fellow workman
and in 1916 he joined the army. He took part in several battles
on the Rumanian front and in July 1917 he was elected to the
regimental committee. Although he did not belong to any
political party, his sympathies lay with the socialists and later
with the Bolsheviks. He regarded the Tsar as a tool of the capi-
talists and thought that prison was the right place for him, but
when he actually saw Nicholas in prison clad in old and worn-
out boots he seems to have felt sorry for him. He formed the
impression that the Tsar was "a kind, simple, frank and talka-
tive person. Sometimes," he said, "I felt that he was going to

THE HOUSE OF SPECIAL PURPOSE

speak to me. He looked as if he would like to talk to us." [4] That, however, he was not allowed to do and from the Bolshevik point of view, the precaution was undoubtedly a sensible one.

Paul Medvedev was also thirty years old at the time of the Tsar's arrival in Ekaterinburg. He had a job in the Sissert Works and owned a house nearby. He was called up for the army in September 1914 but was demobilized within two months because his work was concerned with the production of munitions. He joined the Bolshevik Party in April 1917 as the majority of the men in his factory did at that time. For three months he paid one per cent of his wages into party funds but after that he gave up his membership. In January 1918 he enlisted in the Red Army and took part in some confusing and inconclusive fighting around Troitzk which, according to his descriptions, consisted mainly of wandering about aimlessly. In April 1918 he returned to Ekaterinburg on leave. In May, he volunteered for the guard at Ipatiev's house. Like Yakimov, his acknowledged motive was to earn good money for what was regarded as soft work. Unlike Yakimov, however, he was quite unmoved by the plight of the imperial family.

Such were the elite of the guard at Ipatiev's house. One of the juniors, Philip Proskuriakov, was seventeen when he embarked on his new job. His father advised him not to take it on but he was anxious to see the Tsar and to earn the four hundred rubles a month which was the sum offered in compensation. Such men and their commandant Avdeiev, whether they felt an occasional pang of conscience or not, were the instruments of the persecution to which the imperial family had to submit. But in the Bolshevik hierarchy they were only small fry, nor in the Bolshevik scheme of things were the humiliations which they inflicted upon their prisoners of any great significance. In higher quarters more important plans were being hatched. These were influenced and accelerated by the advance of the Czechoslovak Legion and possibly, in some more obscure way, by the attitude of the Germans.

The most important and the most powerful man in the Ekaterinburg area was Goloshchekin. He had been born in the Vitebsk district in 1876 and had undertaken a dental training. Politically he was a tenacious extremist, and he had played a prominent part in the organization of the revolutionary upheavals of 1905. As a result he had been arrested and imprisoned. Subsequently he escaped but was arrested again in Moscow in 1909, and was exiled to Siberia. Again he escaped and this time fled abroad, where he joined Lenin. In 1912 Goloshchekin was elected to the Central Executive of the Bolshevik Party, in which he was known as "Philip." He returned to Russia and once more was immediately arrested. After the revolution in 1917, Goloshchekin became a virtual dictator in the area of the Ural Mountains. He had recruited and organized a considerable army from among the workers in the local factories and from a medley of nationalities—usually described by the local people as "Lettons"—who for one reason or another found themselves in Siberia. Several of these so-called Lettons were actually Hungarians who, until recently, had been prisoners of war but no one really knew with any precision who the Lettons were. The only certain thing about the majority of them was that they were not Russians.

There can be little doubt that Goloshchekin gave, or at least authorized, the orders which led to the interception of the Tsar when he was traveling with Yakovlev and which, in turn, led to the transfer of the rest of the family from Tobolsk to Ekaterinburg. He also was the power behind the regime in the House of Special Purpose, but in the exercise of power he was an agent rather than a source. Goloshchekin was on intimate terms and in constant touch with Sverdlov, the Chairman of the Central Executive Committee in Moscow.

At the beginning of July 1918 Goloshchekin went to Moscow, where he stayed with Sverdlov. There were important things to discuss and a crisis to be dealt with. The fifth All-Russian Congress of Soviets was in session and at it the Bolshevik Party was defending the policy of peace with Germany. The social revolutionary element took a different view. It demanded a resumption of the war against Germany and when the proposal was voted down by the Bolsheviks, determined to attempt a *coup d'état*. On July 6th, two social revolutionary agents—Blumkin and Andreev—sought and gained admission to the German embassy. They asked to see the ambassador on important business. When he at last received them, they drew and fired their revolvers and also detonated a bomb. That was the end of Count Mirbach.

The assassination was intended to precipitate the outbreak of war between Russia and Germany. It was synchronized with risings organized by the social revolutionaries to overthrow the Bolsheviks in Moscow and Petrograd. But neither object was achieved. The Germans, whose last great offensive in France had now failed, were hardly in a position to undertake another in Russia, and the social revolutionary risings were suppressed within a few days. On July 9th the session of the All-Russian Congress of Soviets was resumed with the Bolsheviks in a stronger position than ever before.

Consolidation at the center was accompanied, however, by what looked like disintegration at the perimeters. As far as Siberia was concerned, this was of particular concern to Goloshchekin. Ekaterinburg itself was already threatened by the advance of the Czechoslovak Legion. The time was obviously approaching when the imperial prisoners would have to be removed from Ipatiev's house or when something else would have to be done about them. No doubt, Goloshchekin discussed the possibilities with Sverdlov. Evidently it was decided that the plan which was adopted could not be entrusted to Avdeiev, the commandant in the House of Special Purpose. Accordingly he was charged with the theft of the personal possessions of the prisoners and dismissed. On July 4th, a new commandant was appointed. Already he had been seen several times in the House of Special Purpose. Now he was in charge of it. His name was Yurovsky. "Decidedly," Nicholas wrote in his diary, "this individual pleases us less and less." [5]

Jacob Yurovsky, thirty years old at the time of his appointment as commandant of Ipatiev's house, was born in Tomsk where his father had settled after being exiled to Siberia for the offense of armed robbery. There he attended the Jewish school but he did not complete his education. Instead he apprenticed himself to a local clockmaker and later set up in that business on his own account. In 1904, he married a divorced woman but soon afterward he went abroad and spent about a year in Berlin. During that time, he abandoned the Jewish faith and adhered to the Lutheran. He lived for a time in Southern Russia and then returned to Tomsk where he re-established his clockmaking business. He did well and became prosperous, though he could barely read or write. He had revolutionary sympathies and these got him into trouble with the police in 1912. Afterward he went into photographic business. On the outbreak of war he was called up and posted as a medical orderly at a hospital in Ekaterinburg. He acquired a considerable interest in medical matters.

In 1917, Yurovsky was among the first in Ekaterinburg to declare for the Bolsheviks and after the second revolution in November he became a member of Ekaterinburg Soviet, a commissar for justice, and an officer of some kind in the secret political police force, known as the *Tcheka,* which had its local headquarters in the Hotel America. Dr. Deverenko remembered that on an occasion in June 1918 when he went to Ipatiev's house to treat the Tsarevitch, who had developed a tumor on the leg, he saw Yurovsky there. He also remembered that Yurovsky had shown a considerable interest in the Tsarevitch's case.

At the beginning of July, Yurovsky came again to the House of Special Purpose. This time he was accompanied by Belobdorov, the President of Regional Soviet of the Urals. Belobdorov announced that Avdeiev had been dismissed and that his place would be taken by Yurovsky with a man named Nikulin as his principal assistant. Yurovsky immediately assumed the command. He made an exhaustive inspection of the whole house. He expelled a number of Avdeiev's hangers-on who were still there and then he summoned Medvedev, the senior guard of the Sissert group, and questioned him closely about the positions of all the sentry posts.

A few days later, ten new sentries arrived. They were called Lettons but it was noticed that Yurovsky often addressed them in German. It was believed that they belonged to the *Tcheka* organization and that they had come from the Hotel America. Only these new men were allowed to guard the sentry posts inside the house. The others were now confined to the posts outside and the only man who had served under Avdeiev who was now allowed inside the house was Medvedev. The others thought that he had found some way of ingratiating himself with Yurovsky. At any rate, he continued to occupy the commandant's room on the first floor, which he now shared with Yurovsky's assistant, Nikulin, and also, apparently, sometimes with the latter's mistress. Yurovsky himelf slept elsewhere. The ten "Lettons" were quartered downstairs and the other sentries, the men from the Zlokazov and Sissert factories, slept in Popov's house on the opposite side of the road. Within a few days of Yurovsky taking over as commandant, a completely new system of guarding the imperial prisoners had been put into operation. The fact was reported to Goloshchekin in Moscow by Belobdorov in Ekaterinburg.

The new regime was even more stringent than the old. One of the regulations now imposed upon the prisoners forbade them to look out of the windows, and when the Grand Duchess Anastasia defied it a sentry below fired and narrowly missed her. Priests, however, were still admitted from time to time to conduct services. One of them, Father Storojev, noticed a difference in the bearing of the prisoners after the arrival of Yurovsky. On an earlier occasion, he had thought that the family was in good heart. The Tsarevitch, who lay on a bed, looked exceedingly ill. His face was absolutely colorless and looked almost transparent but his eyes were clear and lively and he watched everything with the utmost interest. The whole family joined lustily in the singing. On the second occasion, on July

14th, ten days after Yurovsky's arrival, Father Storojev formed a different impression. The Tsarevitch this time was in an armchair and seemed to be slightly better. But he was listless and the rest of the family looked glum and distracted. None of them joined in the singing. Nor can they have been cheered by the fact that for some reason the ceremony was conducted in the form of a funeral service.

In spite of the increased stringency of their conditions, the prisoners were still allowed out for exercise in the garden. On July 16th at about four o'clock in the evening, Yakimov, the senior guard of the Zlokazov group, saw the Tsar and his daughters walking there. At about the same time a mining prospector named Fessenko encountered Yurovsky near some disused mines in the middle of a forest five or six miles to the northwest of Ekaterinburg. Yurovsky wanted to know if a truck with a load of about eight hundred pounds would be able to reach those mines or whether it would get bogged down on the way.

XI

The Special Purpose

WHILE Yurovsky was making his inspection of the approaches to the disused mines in the forest to the northwest of Ekaterinburg, Goloshchekin was returning to that town from Moscow. When he arrived he must have found cause to congratulate himself upon the choice of Yurovsky as the commandant of the House of Special Purpose. The plan which had been made in Moscow had been well and truly prepared for in Ekaterinburg. Such efficiency and such co-ordination were unusual in the Russia of July 1918, and the credit was largely due to the vigor and the resourcefulness of Yurovsky. The result was that the special purpose was now ready for execution—which, for those who had planned it, was as well. There was little time to lose; already by the end of June the Bolshevik leaders had realized that they could not for long hold Ekaterinburg against the advance of the Czechoslovak Legion and the White Army which was gathering around it. The Red Army in Siberia was not yet an effective force.

There were many in Ekaterinburg and in the country around it who were now speculating upon the prospects of this situation. Perhaps, as he strolled with his daughters in the garden of Ipatiev's house on the afternoon of July 16, 1918, the Tsar was also speculating upon the same thing. But if Nicholas looked for a sign in the silent and what by now must have appeared to be the sinister faces of his guards, he can have discerned nothing, for they also did not know the nature of the special purpose. One of its aspects was that it should not be anticipated. Another was that it should not be recorded. The execution of the special purpose was to be sudden, surreptitious, and secret. It was to happen in the dead of night and it was not intended to come to light on the morrow.

But the plan could not be prepared in absolute secrecy. Certain inquiries had to be made in the district and certain arrangements had to be made. Nor was the plan one which could be accomplished by Yurovsky alone, even if only at the last moment he had to take others into his confidence. The special purpose, both in preparation and in execution, left a trail of evidence which has given the outside world the means of knowing what it was not intended to know.

Within a few hours of the Tsar and his daughters coming in from their walk on the afternoon of July 16th, Yurovsky was already taking one of his subordinates, Medvedev, into his confidence. Medvedev was told that all the prisoners were to be shot that night. He was ordered to collect twelve revolvers from the guards and to bring them to Yurovsky's room. He was told to warn the outside guards to disregard any shots they might hear in the night. He was not told on whose authority these orders were issued and he afterward affirmed that he was not interested in that question.

Meanwhile, the prisoners upstairs were eating their evening meal. Their number had been reduced by one on the previous day. Without explanation, the young Sednev, who used to push the Tsarevitch's invalid chair, had been removed. It occurred to the Tsaritsa to wonder if she would ever see the boy again. Those who remained were, therefore, the Tsar and the Tsaritsa, the Grand Duchesses, Olga, Tatiana, Maria, and Anastasia, and the Tsarevitch Alexis, Doctor Botkin, the Tsaritsa's maid, Anna Demidova, the cook, Haritonev, and the valet, Alexis Trupp. Here then were eleven prisoners, seven of whom had committed the crime of being imperial personages and four of whom had committed the apparently equal one of being attached to imperial personages. Certainly they were all in doubt as to their future but they were still unaware of the fact that they had no future. Downstairs this fact was being assured. The twelve revolvers were being collected and loaded. Outside the house the same fact was being obscured. The sentries were posted as usual but the road had been closed to the population of Ekaterinburg. Yurovsky's preparations had been completed. The special purpose now had only to be carried out.

At midnight the prisoners were waked up. They were told that Ekaterinburg was threatened by hostile troops and that they must prepare themselves for a move. About an hour later, they all came downstairs. Yurovsky, accompanied by two or three of his aides, came first. He was followed by the Tsar, who carried his son in his arms, and by the rest of the family and its attendants. Yurovsky led the procession into a room on the ground floor. Three chairs were fetched. The Tsar put his son onto one of them and sat down beside him. The Tsaritsa sat on the other chair. The Grand Duchesses had brought cushions and with these they tried to make their brother and their mother more comfortable. Neither the Tsar nor any of his family nor any of their servants spoke a single word. All appeared to be absolutely calm and all did exactly what they were told. Seven more armed men then entered the room but still none of the prisoners uttered a syllable.

The silence was broken by Yurovsky, who abruptly told the Tsar that he must die. Nicholas had time to speak only a single questioning sentence and to stretch out his arms to his son. The Tsaritsa crossed herself and Anna Demidova took cover behind the useless protection of her pillow. A fusilade followed immediately. In a moment the whole imperial family lay in pools of blood on the floor.

Yurovsky had been the first to shoot and he had shot truly. Nicholas fell, shot through the head and killed instantly by Yurovsky's first bullet. With him and in his father's death clasp lay the Tsarevitch Alexis covered in blood but alive and groaning. Yurovsky aimed again and the child's blood poured out onto the floor to mingle with his father's. The other men, some of them wildly, shot at the other prisoners. The Tsaritsa, three of her daughters, Dr. Botkin, Haritonov, and Trupp fell dead. The Grand Duchess Anastasia and Anna Demidova screamed.

They were violently attacked with bayonets which tore great gashes in the floor. Many more shots were fired and then there was silence again.

On that terrible day the guard Yakimov had as usual done an eight-hour stretch of duty. It began at two o'clock in the afternoon and in the course of it he saw the Tsar and his daughters taking what proved to be their last walk in the garden. At ten o'clock Yakimov was relieved and crossed the road to Popov's house where he went to bed. At about four the next morning as it was just beginning to get light, he and two other guards who shared a room were waked up by the excited voices of two of their comrades named Kleshcheiev and Deriabin who had been on duty outside Ipatiev's house during the night. They said that the Tsar and his family had been killed and that by looking in through windows they had actually witnessed the crime. Deriabin said that he could not hear what Yurovsky said to the Tsar before the shooting began but Kleshcheiev said that his words were: "Nicholas Alexandrovich, your relatives are trying to save you." [1] After the first burst of shooting both men said they heard women's screams. They said that those who survived the bullets were bayoneted and they also said that the Grand Duchess Anastasia was the most injured in this way.

The bodies, according to what these two guards told Yakimov and his friends, were then inspected for signs of life and some further bayoneting took place. A number of jewels were collected from the corpses and were taken upstairs by Yurovsky. Meanwhile, the bodies were wrapped up in sheets and carried out to a truck which was waiting outside. It was driven away by a man named Luhanov who was accompanied by Yurovsky and three of the Lettons who had taken part in the murder. The other Lettons then began to clean up the blood with water and sawdust.

On the following day at two in the afternoon, Yakimov again went on duty at Ipatiev's house. He went up to the commandant's room on the first floor where he found Yurovsky's assistant Nikulin, Medvedev, and two Lettons. They seemed to be preoccupied and depressed; according to what he had been told in the night by Kleshcheiev and Deriabin, all four of them had committed murder some twelve hours earlier. Yurovsky was not there but Yakimov noticed valuable jewelry on his table. The door leading to the room of the imperial family was shut as usual but Yakimov saw their dog sitting beside it and waiting to be let in. Medvedev told Yakimov that the Lettons had done the actual shooting, but no one seemed to know what had become of the bodies.

The guard Proskuriakov had also been on sentry duty outside Ipatiev's house on July 16th. When he was relieved he went out drinking with another guard named Stolov. They had just been paid and when they returned to Popov's house at dusk both were in poor condition—so much so, indeed, that Medvedev had them locked up in the bathroom. They were due to go on duty again at five the next morning but at three they were waked by Medvedev and taken across to Ipatiev's house. Proskuriakov described the ground-floor room to which they were taken. "There was," he said, "a cloud of powder smoke in the room, which smelt strongly of gunpowder. In the back room with the barred window, close to the storeroom, the walls and floor were pierced by bullets—there was also blood, and there were splashes and spots of blood on the walls and pools of blood on the floor—it was obvious," Proskuriakov said, "that just before our arrival a large number of people had been shot in the room with the barred window." [2] This was the mess which Proskuriakov and Stolov were told to clean up with water and sawdust. They did not make a good job of their work and if the intention was to conceal the fact that this was the room in which the murders had been committed, it failed. Many traces of human blood were left in that horrible place.

Medvedev told Proskuriakov that he had been in the room with Belobdorov and Nikulin when Yurovsky read what he described as a "protocol" to the Tsar. Nicholas had apparently asked, "What does all this mean?" and Yurovsky had replied by pointing his revolver at the Tsar and saying "This! Your race must cease to live." Medvedev described to Proskuriakov the shooting which had followed. He said that he himself had fired three times at the Tsar and many times at the other prisoners.

Within an hour or so of the murders, the secret was out. Some of the murderers, and especially Medvedev, seem to have talked freely about it, and naturally those who heard these accounts did not keep them to themselves. By midday on July 17th there were several who had not taken part in the crime who knew that it had been committed. Not all were pleased by what they heard and some were frightened. But the fact of the murders did not come to outside knowledge simply through the process of loose talk. Other signs of it came out in other ways.

To the northwest of Ekaterinburg, there lay a remote village named Koptiaki. It was remote not on account of its distance from Ekaterinburg—which was little more than ten miles—but because of the nature of the country around it. Koptiaki was near the Isset Lake and it was enclosed on all sides by a forest which reached to within a mile or two of Ekaterinburg. The population was small, primitive, and little affected by the pas·sage of time. Some of the people made their living from fish which they sold in Ekaterinburg. This business brought them along the road which passed southward through the forest and toward Ekaterinburg. After a mile or so and in the heart of the forest, this road came to the area known as the "Four Brothers" —so called because of four particularly striking pine trees which had once stood there. Off the road and to its west there were at this point a number of disused iron-ore mines. Several were full of water and all had become densely overgrown with vegetation and trees. These were the mines in which the prospector Fessenko had been interested and which, as he knew, had also been inspected by Yurovsky. Farther to the south and still within the forest there was a level crossing by which the road

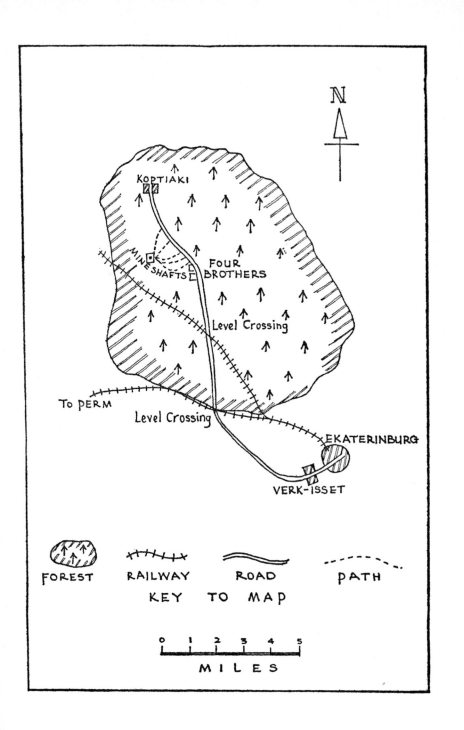

N

KOPTIAKI

MINE SHAFTS

FOUR
BROTHERS

Level Crossing

To PERM

Level Crossing

EKATERINBURG

VERK-ISSET

FOREST   RAILWAY   ROAD   PATH

KEY   TO   MAP

0   1   2   3   4   5

MILES

crossed the railway from Ekaterinburg to Petrograd and still farther to the south, on the edge of the forest, there was a second level crossing by which it passed the railway line to Moscow. Here the road curved in a southeasterly direction, passed through the suburb of Verk-Isset and entered Ekaterinburg.

Very early on the morning of July 17th one of the Koptiaki peasants, Anastasia Zykova, accompanied by her son, Nicholas, and his wife, Marie, set out along this road to sell their fish in Ekaterinburg. By first light they had reached the Four Brothers but there they were met by an unusual sight. They saw several vehicles surrounded by Red guards on horseback. Some of these soldiers galloped toward them, ordered them to turn homeward and not to look around as they went. Two of the guards accompanied them for some distance and were evidently very anxious to see that the three peasants lost no time in getting home. They did as they were told but when they got back to Koptiaki their story aroused considerable interest. The peasants were about to harvest their hay and they feared that what Anastasia Zykova had seen might portend a battle around their village between Whites and Reds. Three of them and an ex-officer who had been in hiding in Koptiaki determined to find out what was happening and they set off immediately along the way from which Anastasia Zykova had just returned.

When they got to the Four Brothers they noticed new wheel tracks leading off the road along a path which led to the disused mines. They started to follow them but were immediately confronted by a Red guard who was armed with a gun, a saber, and a number of grenades. He ordered them to turn back and immediately afterward road blocks were set up both to the north and to the south of the Four Brothers. These were removed on the morning of July 19th.

Meanwhile, in Ekaterinburg, some people knew that on July 17th, the day on which Anastasia Zykova had been turned back, a hundred and ninety kilograms of sulphuric acid and large quantities of benzene had been procured by the Bolshevik authorities on the orders of one of their commissars named

Voikev. Others knew that during the night of July 18th a badly bloodstained truck had been brought back to a garage in Eka-terinburg. On the morning of July 19th Goloshchekin was seen coming back to Ekaterinburg from the direction of the Four Brothers by the keeper of the southern of the two level cross-ings. Whatever had been going on at the disused mines had taken several days, was intended to be completely secret, and had been completed by the morning of July 19th.

On that day Sverdlov caused a public announcement to be made in Moscow. It said that the Tsar had been executed but that his wife and children had been evacuated to another prison in a more secure part of the country. On July 20th Sverdlov had a telephone conversation with the authorities in Ekaterin-burg and after it Goloshchekin announced to the local Soviet that Nicholas II had been shot and that his family had been evacuated. On the following day this news was posted up in the streets of Ekaterinburg.

These announcements were similarly false and they were known to be false by those who made them, and in Ekaterin-burg by a number of others as well. On July 17th, Belobdorov, the president of the Ural Soviet, had sent a coded telegram to the secretary of the Committee of People's Commissars in Mos-cow. The cipher groups represented the following Russian words:

Peredaite Sverdlovoutchto vse semeistvo postigla ta je outchast tchto i glavo offitsialno semiia pogibnet pri evakousatsii.[3]

In English, this meant "Inform Sverdlov that the whole family has shared the fate of its head. Officially they will perish in the evacuation." Evidently, however, the Soviet authorities did not think that the time was ripe to announce that they had killed not only the Tsar, but also his wife and children, Dr. Botkin, and three servants. And even if they had done so, they would still have been admitting much less than the truth. Within a few hours of his own death, many other relatives of Nicholas II were also murdered, some of them even more horribly than himself, and those who survived did so by the grace not of the Russians but of the Germans. If Yurovsky really did tell Nicholas that his race must cease to live, he was, as far as the Romanov family was concerned, accurately pronouncing the policy of the Bolshevik government which he served.

Once more and for the last time, fate had held out an unkind hand to Nicholas II, but as if to justify, or to merit, his lifelong and pessimistic resignation, it did so by the narrowest margin in time. Within three days of the murders, the White Army captured Tiumen from the Bolsheviks, and on July 25, 1918, it entered Ekaterinburg. Those who, if they could, would have rescued the imperial family now had the task of investigating its disappearance.

Anyone who entered it could see that murder had been done in the room with a barred window on the ground floor of Ipatiev's house. But who had been murdered was not obvious and was not easily found out. Murder cannot be established without the production of bodies or remains of them, and of these there was no sign. All sorts of rumors were circulating and all sorts of depositions were made to the White authorities but their investigation was initially neither exhaustive nor systematic and no conclusion could be reached. Some of the "witnesses" examined were, in fact, Bolshevik agents left behind by the retreating Reds. Their evidence supported the official Bolshevik announcements to the effect that the Tsar had been executed and his wife and children evacuated.

Was it possible that the Tsar of all the Russias who had reigned for seventeen years in the twentieth century could simply disappear and that his wife and children could disappear without it ever being known to history what had happened to them? It seemed at first that Yurovsky had done his work so well that this indeed might be the case. But really Yurovsky had not done his work so well. A mass of isolated items of evidence were gradually pieced together and, as a result of what may well be one of the outstanding detective stories of history, the almost certain truth was extracted from obscurity and deception.

One of the principal reasons for this lay in the actions of the peasants at Koptiaki who, it will be remembered, had been curious about what was going on at the Four Brothers between July 17th and 19th. On July 27th two of them, Papine and Alpherov, came to Verk-Isset and told the White military authorities there of the strange things which had been happening in the forest. As a result of their report these authorities sent the forester Riednikov and a party of peasants to examine the area of the disused mines. On July 30th the judge of instruction, Nametkine, accompanied by Dr. Derevenko who had treated the Tsarevitch, Chemodurov, a former valet of the Tsar's, and a number of officers inspected the same area. A few days later, in the presence of Magnitski, the vice-procurator of the Ekaterinburg Tribunal, one of the disused pits was reopened.

As a result, though not all at once, a series of remarkable finds were made. They included the buckle of the Tsar's belt, a piece of his military cap, the frame which had encased his miniature of the Tsaritsa, a pair of the Tsaritsa's earrings, identifiable pieces of her dress, the glass of her spectacles, and a human finger, believed to be her own. Some buttons from the Tsarevitch's uniform were discovered as also were many other odds and ends which had belonged to him. Bits of necklaces, shoes, buttons, and other objects known to have belonged to the Grand Duchesses and a set of false teeth belonging to Dr. Botkin were found. There was evidence, in the shape of six metal corset busks, that *six* women had been stripped. A number of human bones were also discovered.

Nearly all these objects had been touched by fire, the bones had been partly dissolved by acid and some of them bore the marks of a sharp instrument. Others had bullets embedded in them. This evidence was substantially conclusive. It was clear that the victims had been brought to the area of the mines, stripped, cut up, and burned. An attempt had been made to dissolve their bones in acid and the remains had been thrown down the mine shaft. There could hardly be any doubt that these remains were all that was left of the Tsar, his son, Dr. Botkin, Haritonev and *six* women, the Tsaritsa, her maid Anna Demidova, and her four daughters.

But the evidence, though substantially so, was not absolutely conclusive. The human remains could be identified not from what they themselves were. They could only be identified from the possessions found with them and from the further evidence which came to light about the events which had preceded this frightful piece of butchery. Innumerable witnesses of strange events during the night of July 16 to 17, 1918, were minutely questioned by the White investigators. Telegrams and other documents were impounded, examined and, in one case only after two years of endeavor, decoded. A number of former guards at the House of Special Purpose duly fell into White hands and were questioned. Among them were Yakimov and Proskuriakov and, as was even more important, Medvedev himself.

Medvedev was made a prisoner when Perm was captured by the Whites in February 1919. By that time he had only a month in which to live, for in March 1919 he died of typhus, but that month was of immense significance in the investigation of the imperial tragedy. Medvedev was the only person interrogated who admitted to having actually accompanied Yurovsky when he led the Tsar and his family into the room with the barred window in the very early hours of the morning of July 17, 1918. He claimed that just before the shooting, he was sent out to see that nothing was amiss outside, but he said that when he came back the Tsarevitch was still alive.

Even if Medvedev's defensive story was true, he was undoubtedly the most highly informed witness who ever fell into the hands of the White investigators. It is, in fact, more than probable that he was himself one of the murderers. His account of what happened in that room is obviously the most important that has ever been given to the outside world. Only one man could have given more important evidence and that was Yurovsky himself. But Yurovsky, after leaving for Moscow, seems never to have been heard of again. Apparently he disappeared as completely as he had intended the Tsar to disappear.

But the evidence of men like Medvedev, Yakimov, and Proskuriakov was the evidence, at worst, of assassins and, at best, of accomplices. Moreover, it was the evidence of frightened men and, as such, it was obviously unreliable. Nevertheless, all the accounts given by these men substantially confirmed each other, they fitted with the material evidence found in Ipatiev's house, with the documentary evidence found elsewhere, and with the remains found in the area of the Four Brothers. Many accepted historical facts rest on less secure foundations than those concerning the death of Tsar Nicholas II, the Tsaritsa Alexandra, the Tsarevitch Alexis, and the four Grand Duchesses Olga, Tatiana, Marie, and Anastasia.

Even so, the death of princes in mysterious circumstances often produces a crop of impostors, for often there are crowns, power, fortunes and at least notoriety at stake. So it was with the English Princes in the Tower, the victims of their uncle King Richard III. So it was with the Dauphin, the supposed Louis XVII, the victim of the French Revolution, and so it was with the imperial family of Russia, the victims of the Bolshevik revolution. A boy claiming to be the Tsarevitch Alexis soon turned up in Siberia. Later another appeared with the same claim in Baghdad and for an instant or two some with varying degrees of likeness to Nicholas II enjoyed their moments of expectation. No one, however, was for long in doubt that the fate of Nicholas and his son had been sealed on that terrible night in the middle of July 1918. Nor can anyone doubt that they shared their fate with the Tsaritsa, whom, apparently, no one has dared or wished to impersonate, and the Grand Duchesses Olga, Tatiana, and Marie. But about the youngest daughter, the Grand Duchess Anastasia, there is still, after forty years, a lingering doubt left to preserve the imperial tragedy and to shatter the life of a poor woman who now lives in the Black Forest.

The last legacy of the Special Purpose has been the agonizing division sown by doubt between friends and between relatives and no less between sympathizers.

Epilogue

Now are the mighty fallen and how little is their fall regretted? Within a few months of the murder of Nicholas II, the Austro-Hungarian and the German empires followed the Russian and crashed into the dust. War, once the sport of kings, had, in the end, been the death of them. Yet war had been made total and terrible, not by kings, but by revolutions and democracy. Liberalism, which had striven against Romanov, Hapsburg, and Hohenzollern, was in turn to be confronted by Stalin, Mussolini, and Hitler. Such was one of history's inexhaustible ironies. Part of it engulfed the life and encompassed the death of Nicholas II.

Nothing he ever did, it seems, achieved its intended, and often well intended, purpose. His marriage was for love, but its result was a lifelong agony for the lovers. His reign was for the order of Alexander III, but its end was a revolution. His abdication was to save the throne, preserve the armies, and protect his son. Its outcome was the collapse of the throne, the disintegration of the armies and, within minutes of his own, the death of his son.

Nicholas II, in fact, was never mighty at all. He was only the great-great-great-grandson of Catherine the Great and to be that at the beginning of the twentieth century was, indeed, to have been born at the time of which it was written:

> Let darkness and the shadow of death stain it; let a cloud dwell upon it; let the blackness of the day terrify it.

Nicholas exerted little influence over his times and less over his own destiny. His color was pale, his expression was dreamy, his smile was melancholy, and his gestures were timid.[1] He knew how to pray but not how to fight. He knew how to yield but not how to resist. He knew how to obey but not how to command. He knew how to die but not how to live. His defects as a sovereign might have been his qualities as an ordinary man, but neither his simplicity and his humility nor even his abdication could bring the ordinary life within his grasp. In that lay the tragedy of his existence.

His death made no difference to history and the news of it was received with indifference by the masses of the Russian people, but surely the memory of the former Tsar, who endured his persecution and met his death with Christian courage, deserves better than the futile flattery of courtiers, the gibes of frustrated liberals, and the abuse of communists. Nor was the Christian courage of Nicholas II his alone. Faith in God was the sustaining force and the redeeming feature of him and his wife. It was shared by their innocent children.

When the guards of Ipatiev's house cleared out, they took many things with them but in their haste they overlooked others. Among the latter were some sheets of paper on which in the handwriting of Nicholas' eldest daughter, the Grand Duchess Olga, the following prayer was copied:

> Give patience, Lord, to us Thy children,
> In these dark, stormy days to bear
> The persecution of our people,
> The tortures falling to our share.

> Give strength, Just God, to us who need it,
> The persecutors to forgive,
> Our heavy, painful cross to carry
> And Thy great meekness to achieve.

> When we are plundered and insulted,
> In days of mutinous unrest,
> We turn for help to Thee, Christ-Saviour,
> That we may stand the bitter test.

EPILOGUE

Lord of the World, God of Creation,
Give us Thy blessing through our prayer,
Give peace of heart to us, O Master,
This hour of utmost dread to bear.

And on the threshold of the grave
Breathe power divine into our clay
That we, Thy children, may find strength
In meekness for our foes to pray.[2]

Notes

PROLOGUE

1. Job, III, 1-5.
2. Nicholas to Marie Feodorovna. April 28, 1896. *Bing:* p. 114.
3. Nicholas Diary. January 2, 1892. *Pares:* p. 33.
4. Nicholas to Marie Feodorovna. April 22, 1894. *Bing:* p. 75.
5. Ditto. P. 76.
6. Alexandra to Nicholas. January 15, 1916. *Slovo:* p. 249.
7. Nicholas to Marie Feodorovna. June 26, 1894. *Bing:* p. 82.
8. Nicholas Diary. October 27, 1894. *Dnevnik, Slovo:* p. 83.
9. *Nicolson:* p. 57.

CHAPTER I

1. Nicholas to Marie Feodorovna. November 1, 1905. *Bing:* p. 188.
2. Ditto. November 23, 1905. P. 194.
3. Ditto. December 21, 1905. P. 200.
4. Ditto. October 18, 1905. *Léon:* pp. 62-3. (Trans. from French.)
5. *Mossolov:* pp. 139-40.
6. Ditto. P. 139.
7. *Buxhoeveden:* pp. 108-9.
8. *Buchanan:* II, p. 89. (Trans. from French.)
9. *Buxhoeveden:* p. 109.
10. Nicholas Diary. November 14, 1905. *Pares:* p. 137.

CHAPTER II

1. *Trotsky:* p. 73.
2. *Pares:* p. 143.
3. Ditto. P. 154.

CHAPTER III

1. *Trotsky:* p. 59.
2. *Cruttwell:* p. 171.
3. *Buchanan:* I, p. 238.

4. *Pares:* p. 270.
5. Alexandra to Nicholas. July 8, 1915. *Slovo:* pp. 110-11.
6. Ditto. September 4, 1915. Pp. 113-14.

CHAPTER IV

1. *Ludendorff:* I, p. 171.
2. *Radziwill:* p. 226.
3. Alexandra to Nicholas. July 5, 1915. *Slovo:* p. 106.
4. Ditto.
5. Ditto. September 19, 1915. P. 144.
6. Ditto. June 28, 1915. P. 96.
7. Ditto. June 29, 1915. P. 96.
8. Ditto. January 22, 1916. P. 261. The Tsaritsa habitually and accurately referred to Goremykin as the "Old Man."
9. Ditto. P. 260. The Tsaritsa usually referred to Rasputin as "our Friend" or "our Fr.," sometimes as Gregory, but never as Rasputin. There had been a suggestion that Stürmer should change his name so as to look less German.
10. Nicholas to Alexandra. November 22, 1916. *Hynes:* p. 296.
11. Alexandra to Nicholas. November 23, 1916. *Slovo:* p. 438. Presumably by a slip of the pen, the Tsaritsa actually wrote "thinks will be difficult."
12. Nicholas to Alexandra. November 23, 1916. *Hynes:* pp. 297-8.
13. Alexandra to Nicholas. November 24, 1916. *Slovo:* pp. 439-40.
14. Ditto. November 25, 1916. P. 442.

CHAPTER V

1. Nicholas to Alexandra. December 17, 1916. *Hynes:* p. 299.
2. Alexandra to Nicholas. December 17, 1916. *Slovo:* pp. 442-3.
3. Nicholas to Alexandra. December 18, 1916. *Hynes:* p. 299. The Tsarevitch was with his father at headquarters.
4. Ditto. December 31, 1916. P. 312.
5. Alexandra to Nicholas. December 30, 1916. *Slovo:* p. 461.
6. Ditto. October 23, 1915. P. 195.
7. Ditto. November 25, 1915. P. 217.
8. *Wilson Diary:* I. February 16, 1917. P. 319.
9. Ditto. February 18, 1917. P. 320.
10. Ditto. February 3, 1917. P. 315.

11. Ditto. January 31, 1917. P. 314.
12. Nicholas Diary. March 7, 1917. *Krasnaya Gazeta.* (Trans. from Russian.)
13. Nicholas to Alexandra. March 11, 1917. *Hynes:* pp. 316-7.
14. Ditto. P. 317.
15. Alexandra to Nicholas. March 10, 1917. *Sergeyev:* p. 218. (Trans. from Russian.)
16. Ditto. March 11, 1917. P. 221.
17. Nicholas to Alexandra. March 13, 1917. *Hynes:* p. 318.
18. Ditto.
19. Ditto. March 15, 1917. P. 319.
20. Nicholas Diary. March 15, 1917. *Krasnaya Gazeta.* (Trans. from Russian.)

CHAPTER VI

1. Nicholas Diary. March 16, 1917. *Krasnaya Gazeta.* (Trans. from Russian.)
2. *Sokolov:* p. 20. (Trans. from French.)
3. Alexandra to Nicholas. March 16, 1917. *Sergeyev:* p. 232. (Trans. from Russian.)

CHAPTER VII

1. *Kerensky:* p. 122.
2. Ditto.
3. Ditto.
4. Ditto. P. 123.
5. Deposition of Colonel Kobylinsky. April 6-10, 1919. *Wilton:* p. 177.
6. Nicholas Diary. March 23, 1917. *Payot 1914–1918:* p. 96. (Trans. from French.)
7. Extract from letter: Bertie to Foreign Secretary. April 22, 1917. *Lloyd George:* I, p. 975.
8. Ditto.
9. Ditto. P. 976.
10. *Buxhoeveden:* p. 313.
11. Gilliard Diary. March 17, 1918. *Gilliard:* p. 256.
12. Ditto.

CHAPTER VIII

1. *Benckendorff:* pp. 97-8.
2. Nicholas Diary. July 21, 1917. *Payot 1914–1918:* p. 130. (Trans. from French.)
3. *Buxhoeveden:* p. 306.
4. *Benckendorff:* p. 112.
5. *Buxhoeveden:* p. 327.
6. Gilliard Diary. April 22, 1918. *Gilliard:* p. 259.

CHAPTER IX

1. Gilliard Diary. April 25, 1918. *Gilliard:* p. 260.
2. Ditto. P. 261.
3. Ditto.
4. *Sokolov:* p. 77. (Trans. from French.)
5. Gilliard Diary. April 25, 1918. *Gilliard:* p. 262.
6. *Gilliard:* p. 269.

CHAPTER X

1. From the prayer of the Grand Duchess Olga. See p. 176.
2. Nicholas Diary. July 4, 1918. *Payot 1914–1918:* p. 213. (Trans. from French.)
3. Rodzianko: *Tattered Banners:* p. 139.
4. Deposition of Yakimov, May 7-11, 1919. *Wilton:* p. 274.
5. Nicholas Diary. July 11, 1918. *Payot 1914–1918:* p. 214. (Trans. from French.)

CHAPTER XI

1. Deposition of Yakimov. May 7-11, 1919. *Wilton:* p. 279.
2. Deposition of Proskuriakov. April 1-3, 1919. *Wilton:* p. 303.
3. *Sokolov:* pp. 283-4. A translation into French is given here.

EPILOGUE

1. See the comparison of Nicholas II and George V made by President Poincaré in 1913. *Nicolson:* p. 217.
2. This is the English rendering given in *Kerensky:* pp. 25-6.

Note on Sources

The list of sources which follows is selective and not comprehensive. It has been divided into three general headings: Primary Materials, Memoirs, and Histories. Under primary materials are included diaries and letters of the Tsar, the Tsaritsa, and the Tsar's mother, the Tsaritsa Marie Feodorovna, some other documents, certain depositions, and the report on the judicial inquiry into the death of the imperial family. Under memoirs, whether or not they were written as such, are mainly listed the works of people who knew the Tsar and Tsaritsa personally or who played a part in the events connected with their life and death. The term "histories" is self-explanatory.

The primary materials have suffered various degrees of removal from the originals in the processes of publication and, in most cases, of translation into English, French, or Russian. The *Slovo* edition of the Tsaritsa's letters to the Tsar between 1914 and 1916 are, however, published in the original English in which they were written. The Hynes edition of the Tsar's letters to her during approximately the same period are, on the other hand, translated into English from the official Russian translation which, in turn, was made from the original English. Even so, the quality and the volume of primary material which is available in published form is remarkable. It need hardly be emphasized that it would be much less had it not been for the desire of the Bolshevik authorities to show these things to the world. There is every cause to believe that all the primary materials listed here are entirely genuine, though in some respects they are not always complete.

The memoirs, as might be expected, are of extremely various quality. They range from the highly inaccurate to the fairly true and, of course, none of them are wholly impartial. Those who served the Tsar as also those who played a part in his downfall are hardly likely to view the event in a dispassionate light. Some, in addition, clearly have bad memories. Such sources have to be used with care but they are, nevertheless, indispensable.

The histories which throw light upon this particular aspect of the subject are not numerous and they too are of somewhat various quality. By far the most important is Sir Bernard Pares' masterly work on the fall of the Russian Monarchy which was published in 1939 after a lifetime of study and of firsthand experience.

In the text I have followed the principle of citing sources specifically only when making an actual quotation from them. For this purpose, I have used abbreviated references which are indicated in the list which follows. In quoting from the letters and diaries of the Tsar and the Tsaritsa I have omitted their frequent underlinings.

I. PRIMARY MATERIALS

"Depositions of Eye Witnesses interrogated in the course of the judicial enquiry into the assassination of the Imperial family." See under Memoirs, *Wilton*.

Dnevnik (Diary) of Nicholas II. Slovo, Berlin, 1924. In Russian. Cited as *Dnevnik, Slovo*.

Journal Intime de Nicholas II 1890–1917. (Extracts.) Trans. into French by A. Pierre. Payot, Paris, 1925.

Journal Intime de Nicholas II Juillet 1914–Juillet 1918. Trans. into French by M. Bénouville and A. Kaznakov. Payot, Paris, 1934. Cited as *Payot, 1914–1918*.

Krasnaya Gazeta (Red Gazette). *Abdication of Nicholas II. Recollections of Witnesses, Documents*. Ed. by P. E. Scheglov. Intro. by L. Kitayev and M. E. Koltsov. Leningrad, 1927. (In Russian.) Cited as *Krasnaya Gazeta*.

The Letters of the Tsar to the Tsaritsa 1914–1917. Trans. from Russian by A. L. Hynes. Intro. and notes by C. E. Vulliamy. London: John Lane The Bodley Head Ltd. New York: Dodd Mead and Co. 1929. Cited as *Hynes*.

The Letters of Tsar Nicholas and Empress Marie. Ed. by Edward J. Bing. Intro. by R. H. Bruce Lockhart. (Selected from five hundred letters 1879–1917.) Ivor Nicholson and Watson, 1937. Cited as *Bing*.

Lettres de Nicholas II et de sa Mère. Traduction, Intro. et Notes de

Paul L. Léon. (May 18, 1905–November 10, 1906 O.S.) Simon Kra, Paris, 1928, 3rd. Ed. Cited as *Léon.*
Letters of the Tsaritsa to the Tsar 1914–1916. Intro. by Sir Bernard Pares. Duckworth, 1923. (April 24, 1914–December 17, 1916 O.S.) These 404 letters, printed in the original English, were discovered in a black box at Ipatiev's house after the murder. They were originally published by Joseph Hessen in Berlin for Slovo. Cited as *Slovo.*
Perepiska (Correspondence) of Nicholas and Alexandra Romanov 1916–1917. Vol. V. Intro. by M. Pokrovsky. Ed. by A. A. Sergeyev. State Publishing House, Moscow, 1927 Leningrad. (In Russian.) Cited as *Sergeyev.*
Nicolas Sokolov. *Enquête Judiciaire Sur L'Assassinat de la Famille Impériale Russe.* Payot, Paris, 1924. Cited as *Sokolov.* (Sokolov was *Juge d'Instruction* of the Omsk Tribunal.)

II. MEMOIRS

Count Paul Benckendorff. *The Last Days at Tsarskoe Selo.* Trans. by M. Baring. Heinemann, 1927. Cited as *Benckendorff.* (Count Benckendorff was Grand Marshal of the Court of Nicholas II.)
Sir George Buchanan. *My Mission to Russia and Other Diplomatic Memoirs.* 2 Vols. Cassell 1923. Cited as *Buchanan.* (Sir George Buchanan was British Ambassador to Russia 1910–1918.)
P. Bulygin and A. Kerensky. *The Murder of the Romanovs.* Intro. by Sir Bernard Pares. (1) *The Road to Tragedy* by Kerensky, cited as *Kerensky.* (2) *The Sorrowful Quest* by Bulygin. Hutchinson, 1935. (Kerensky was successively Minister of Justice and Prime Minister in the Provisional Government of 1917.)
Baroness Sophie Buxhoeveden. *The Life and Tragedy of Alexandra Feodorovna, Empress of Russia.* Longmans Green and Co., 1930. Cited as *Buxhoeveden* (Baroness Buxhoeveden was a Lady in Waiting to the Tsaritsa.)
Major-General Sir C. E. Callwell. *Field Marshal Sir Henry Wilson Bart., G.C.B., D.S.O. His Life and Diaries.* Preface by Marshal Foch. 2 Vols. Cassell, 1927. Cited as *Wilson Diary.*
P. Gilliard. *Thirteen Years at the Russian Court.* Trans. by F. Appleby Holt. Hutchinson, 1921. Cited as *Gilliard.* (M. Gilliard, who was Swiss, was tutor in French to the Tsarevitch.)

David Lloyd George. *War Memoirs.* 2 Vols. Odhams Press, 1938. Cited as *Lloyd George.*

General Ludendorff. *My War Memories 1914–1918.* 2 Vols. Hutchinson. Cited as *Ludendorff.*

Grand Duchess Marie. *Things I Remember.* Trans. from French and Russian under editorial supervision of Russell Lord. Cassell, 1931. (The Grand Duchess Marie was a daughter of the Grand Duke Paul, a granddaughter of the Tsar Alexander II, and a sister of the Grand Duke Dimitri.)

Sergei Vladimirovitch Markov. *How We Tried to Save the Tsaritsa.* Trans. by F. S. Flint and D. F. Tait. G. P. Putnam's Sons, 1929. (Markov, not to be confused with "Markov II," who was a leader of the supposed escape organization, was a subaltern officer in the Tsaritsa's Own Crimean Cavalry Regiment and was among those who tried to rescue the imperial family.)

General A. A. Mossolov. *At the Court of the Last Tsar.* Ed. by A. A. Pilenco. Trans. by E. W. Dickes. Methuen, 1935. Cited as *Mossolov.* (General Mossolov was Head of the Court Chancellery 1900–1916.)

M. Paléologue. *An Ambassador's Memoirs.* 3 Vols. Trans. by F. A. Holt. Hutchinson, 1923–1925. (M. Paléologue was French ambassador to Russia.)

V. S. Pankratov. *With the Tsar in Tobolsk from Recollections.* Co-operative Publishing Fraternity Buloye, Leningrad, 1925. (In Russian.) (Pankratov was Commissar in charge of the imperial prisoners at Tobolsk in 1918.)

Sir Francis Pridham. *Close of a Dynasty.* Foreword by H.I.H. the Grand Duchess Xenia Alexandrovna. Allan Wingate, 1956. (Vice-Admiral Pridham was First Lieutenant in H.M.S. *Marlborough* in which surviving members of the imperial family, including the Tsaritsa Marie Feodorovna and the Grand Duke Nicholas Nicholaïevitch, were evacuated from Yalta in April 1919.)

Princess Catherine Radziwill. *Nicholas II: The Last of the Tsars.* Cassell, 1931. Cited as *Radziwill.*

M. V. Rodzianko. *The Reign of Rasputin: An Empire's Collapse.* Trans. by Catherine Zvegintzoff. Intro. by Sir Bernard Pares. A. M. Philpot, 1927. (Rodzianko was President of the Imperial Duma.)

Colonel P. Rodzianko. *Tattered Banners:* Seeley Service, 1939.

Major-General Sir John Hanbury-Williams. *The Emperor Nicho-*

las II As I Knew Him. Arthur Humphreys, 1922. (Sir John Hanbury-Williams was head of the British Military Mission to Russia 1914–1917.)

Robert Wilton. *The Last Days of the Romanovs.* Thornton Butterworth, 1920. (Mr. Wilton was Special Correspondent of the *Times* in Russia.) The second part of this volume consists of the depositions of eyewitnesses, for which see above under Primary Materials. Cited as *Wilton.*

III. HISTORIES ETC.

James Bunyan. *Intervention, Civil War and Communism in Russia.* April-December 1918. Johns Hopkins Press, 1936.

C. R. M. F. Cruttwell. *A History of the Great War 1914–1918.* Oxford Clarendon Press, Second Edition, 1936. Cited as *Cruttwell.*

Jean Jacoby. *Le Tsar Nicholas II et la Révolution.* Arthème Fayard et Cie, Paris, 1933.

Harold Nicolson. *King George the Fifth, His Life and Reign.* Constable, 1952. Cited as *Nicolson.*

Sir Bernard Pares. *The Fall of the Russian Monarchy. A' Study of the Evidence.* Cape, 1939. Cited as *Pares.*

Leon Trotsky. *The History of the Russian Revolution.* Trans. by Max Eastman. Victor Gollancz, 1934. Cited as *Trotsky.*

Index

INDEX

Koptiaki, 166, 168
Korovichenko, Colonel, 116, 117, 118
Kotsebue, Colonel, 108, 110, 116
Koulomzino, 147
Kremlin, 50

Lemberg, 53, 54
Lena, 47
Lenin, Nikolai, 55, 107, 116, 119, 132, 142, 156
Lettons, 156, 164
Lichoslavl, 92
Louis IV, Grand Duke, 14, 15
Louis XVI, of France, 21, 123, 124
Louis XVIII, of France, 119
Louis Philippe, 119
Louise of Battenburg, Princess, 29
Loukhomsky, General, 96
Loupin, Peter, 138
Ludendorff, General von, 53
Luhanov, 164
Lvov, Prince, 60, 62, 84, 85, 91, 106, 123

Mackensen, General von, 54
Magnitski, 171
Marie, Grand Duchess, 21, 65, 93, 94, 103, 105, 144, 145, 153, 162, 163, 173
Marie Antoinette, 21
Marie Feodorovna, Tsaritsa, 79, 84, 106, 107, 125, 152
Marie Pavlovna, Grand Duchess, 15, 27, 82
Markov, 134-35
Medvedev, Paul, 154, 155, 159, 162, 165, 166, 172, 173
Michael, Grand Duke, 28, 91, 98, 100
Michael Feodorovitch, Tsar, 151
Mirbach, Count, 135, 157
Mohilev, 57, 60, 62, 69, 70, 71, 72, 78, 87, 89, 90, 92, 95, 96, 104, 106, 107
Moscow, 50-51, 60, 64, 136
Moscow Central Executive Committee, 141-42, 156
Mossolov, General, 29, 72-73
Mussolini, Benito, 175

Nagorny, 108, 149, 150, 153
Nametkine, 171
Napoleon I, 44, 67
Napoleon III, 119

Nicholas II, Tsar, abdication, 96-99, 100, 105; arrest of, 107-10; asylum offered by England, 119-20; betrothal to Princess Alix, 15-17; birth, 13; burial of, 166-72; captivity of, 111-21; children of, 23, 102-04; constitutional reform of, 26, 41; effect of Rasputin's death on, 80-82; exile in Siberia, 122-40; family troubles, 27-28; fatalism of, 14, 26, 31-32, 40, 47, 49; imprisonment in Ekaterinburg, 151-60; influence of Tsaritsa on, 29, 30-32, 71-72, 78-79, 111; investigation by the Bolsheviks, 118-19, 120; isolation of, 33, 63; journey from Tobolsk to Ekaterinburg, 141-50; Kerensky and, 114-16, 123-24; marriage, 17-18; murder of, 161-66; personality of, 20-21, 40; place in history, 175-76; Rasputin's influence on, 46-47; rescue attempts, 133-35, 153-54; during the revolution, 95-99; supreme commander of the army, 55, 57-59, 60-61; Tsar of the Russians, 17; weakness of, 30, 78, 100-01
Nicholas Michaelovitch, Grand Duke, 87, 96
Nicholas Nicholaïevitch, Grand Duke, 26, 52, 53, 57, 58, 67
Nikolsky, 129
Nikulin, 158, 159, 165

Okhrana (secret police), 24, 43, 47
Olga, Grand Duchess, 21, 89, 102, 162, 173, 176
Omsk, 132, 137, 147
Ouspensky Sabor, 51

Palace revolutions, 84
Paley, Princess, 81
Pankratov, 128-29, 130
Papine, 171
Paris, 52, 124
Paul, Grand Duke, 74, 81, 82, 84, 105
Pavlovsk Regiment, 90
Pensa, 132
Perm, 172
Peterhof, 31, 89
Petrograd, 50, 54, 55, 64, 73, 82-83, 84, 85, 87, 89, 90, 91, 94, 122, 123, 126, 136; see also St. Petersburg

INDEX

Ukraine, 131

Vachot, Philippe, 34, 35, 79
Vassilieff, Father, 35
Verk-Isset, 168, 171
Versailles, 123
Viazma, 92
Victoria, Queen, 14, 15, 16, 17, 127
Vilna, 54
Vladimir, Grand Duke, 27
Vladivostok, 132
Voikev, 169
Volynski Regiment, 91
Vyrubova, Anna, 36-37, 43, 45, 77, 84, 94, 108, 116, 118, 133, 138

Walton-on-Thames, 16
Warsaw, 52, 53, 54
White Army, 153, 161, 170, 172
Wilhelm II, Kaiser, 15

Williams, General Sir John Hanbury, 96
Wilson, General Sir Henry, 88-89
Windsor Castle, 16
Winter Palace, St. Petersburg, 24, 28, 29, 50, 94
Witte, Count Sergei Y., 26-27, 29, 41, 55
Wulfurt, Madame, 28

Yakimov, Anatoly, 154-55, 160, 164, 165, 172, 173
Yakovlev, Vassili V., 139-40, 141-47
Yanishev, Father, 16
Yurovsky, Jacob, 48, 157-60, 161, 162, 163, 164, 165, 166, 172, 173
Yusopov, Prince Felix, 74, 75, 81, 82

Zemstva, Council of, 60, 62, 85
Zlokazov, Nicholas, 145

3 95